CREATE YOUR BEST LIFE—KILL THE GRIM REAPER

How to Live Fully
Knowing One Day You Will Die

ANDY + MARY ——————
To THE VERY "BEST"
REST OF YOUR LIFE!
CHARITY,
Duke

DUKE ROBINSON

ISBN: 1463737076
ISBN-13: 9781463737078

Library of Congress Control Number: 2011912685
Createspace, North Charleston, SC

If we are ever to enjoy life, now is the time—not tomorrow, nor next year, nor in some future life after we have died. The best preparation for a better life next year is a full, complete, joyous harmonious life this year.

Thomas Dreier

CONTENTS

The best day of your life is the one on which you decide your life is your own. No apologies or excuses. No one to lean on, rely on, or to blame. The gift is yours—it is an amazing journey–and you alone are responsible for the quality of it. This is the day your life really begins.

Bob Moawad

I've learned that there are very few things that really matter in life–but those few things matter intensely.

William Barclay

Do not seek death. Death will find you. But seek the road which makes death a fulfillment.

Dag Hammarskjöld

Every single thing you do matters. You have been created one of a kind to make a difference. You have within you the power to change the world.

Andy Andrews

Every life is a play in search of a good ending.

Milton Matz

INTRODUCTION

When you finish this book, you will feel more alive than ever before.

The awareness that you will one day die may trouble you, especially whenever you stop running and the noise abates. And if you are typical, you suspect you are not prepared to entertain your final hours bravely and at peace. Whether you're aware of it or not, the grim reaper has a grip on you.

During my nearly forty years as a Presbyterian pastor, I regularly spoke about how to live and die well—in classes, in counseling sessions, in conferences, and over coffee after our Sunday morning celebrations. One Sunday, after I had talked about living your best life, a businessman in his early forties took me aside and said, *I'm living feverishly and it's driving me crazy. I don't know how to stop. And I don't want to live this way till the day I die.*

Many of the adults I spoke with over the years gave the impression they were happy and on top of things. But whenever they felt safe to converse at a deeper level, I kept hearing comments like these:

- *I took on my parents' views of life and they're not working.*

- *When my father retired, I inherited his stressful business. A year later he died of a heart attack. I now don't know what in the world I'm working for.*

- *My girlfriend's brother dropped dead last week at thirty-five. They're still trying to figure out why, but my God ...thirty-five!*

- *I've worked my ass off the past several years and been very success- ful, but I don't think I'm supposed to live this way.*

- *When I was a kid and dying came to mind, I thought of my grand- parents. Now when I'm forced to think about death, it's my own that troubles me.*

- *My mom lingered eight horrible months with cancer metastases. I'm terrified of something like that happening to me.*

These people feared both living and dying poorly. Because of cancer, strokes, heart attacks, natural and human caused disasters, they also were afraid they might die early, before they had a chance to live a full lifetime. After thinking through what it means to be human, and the values and com- mitments we talked about, many bit the bullet, dug in, and attempted—as we used to say—to *get their heads on straight* and *their acts together* about how to live their best possible life.

I've written this book for readers willing to do just that—women and men who don't want to sail rudderless the rest of their lives. They want to steer their own ships with knowledge and wisdom and are willing to do their own think- ing. And, because you've come even this short distance with me, I assume you're this kind of person. I assume too, that when you come to the end of your days you hope you'll be able to say, *I lived my best possible life, and I can face my dying at peace.* When you're finished this book, you'll be better prepared to say that.

Skip the Basics

Let's get this out of the way right now. It will be hard to reflect on your life and eventual death if you don't possess what nearly everyone today deems essential for survival: 1) Work you love, or can stand, that pays the bills; 2) shelter from the elements; 3) reasonable measures of nourishing food; 4) transportation—whether car, bicycle, rapid transit, or taxi; 5) good health and adequate health care; 6) clothing to keep you warm and presentable; 7) a safe social context; and 8) contemporary tools of communication (phone, television, computer).

Yes, some people who don't have all of these things can lead very good lives. My point is, if you haven't taken care of most of them, you'll find it hard to focus on what I'll be covering. I'll be introducing you to different perspectives, attitudes, and habits essential not for you to survive but to *thrive*, which is what you were born to do; and they will require your attention. If you have not yet taken care of two or three of these basics, you may be able to fulfill them as you try to deal with what you read here. Ordinarily, though, to tackle what it takes to live your best possible life, you must first have the basics covered.

That's all I have to say about survival basics. Forget them, if you can.

The Coherent Worldview Issue

One afternoon, I stopped by to see Dale, a longtime friend approaching his eighty-seventh birthday. He'd spent the previous night in the hospital with a high fever, and I was concerned. I found him with his wife, Elsie, and her daughter, Karen, as well as Karen's twenty-something son, Jeremy. After we all said how good it was to hear that antibiotics had kicked Dale's fever, we began talking about life and what a mystery it is.

I mentioned a question raised by a book I'd borrowed from Dale and just been reading: *Do we have trouble living well and facing death because we are sinful, as the Bible suggests, or is it because the species of which we are members has not matured enough?*

The older adults batted a few comments around before Jeremy, who'd been listening intently, said, *My friends and I never have conversations about subjects like this.* After an awkward pause, I said I was sorry to hear that, because with all the astonishing advances in knowledge these days, they could be left without *coherent worldviews* and live unfulfilled lives. Jeremy paused thoughtfully for a moment before replying, *None of my friends has anything like a coherent worldview.* His words didn't surprise me. From my discussions with people such as those I quote on the first two pages, I'd already concluded that this problem is widespread.

By worldview, I'm referring to your understanding of the cosmos, the world you live in, and what it means to be a child of the universe or, if you prefer, a child of God. It's the mental framework that gathers and shapes your views of what we might call *the totality of things,* so that it both determines and reflects what's important to you. Your worldview includes your answers to the big questions that always have challenged humankind, including the most important one I focus on in this book: *What does it take to live your best possible life knowing one day you will die?*

When I speak of a worldview that is *coherent,* I am talking about a collection of interlocking concepts that are generally consistent with one another—that is, they contain no major contradictions. Consistency of thought, of course, is not enough. If you are out of touch with reality, your take on things may be consistent, but *consistently wrong.* An example of wrongheaded consistency, to my mind, is the worldview that says that pain, death, and evil are not real, but are figments of the imagination. In order for your worldview to be coherent, it needs not only to be consistent but it also must fit *the facts of our mortal existence as we know them.* And because just yesterday we lacked much of the knowledge with which we must reckon today, we must regularly reconstruct our worldviews so they square with what we now know to be real.

In this book, I lay out in philosophical and practical terms some of what it takes to construct a coherent view of reality as we know it today and to live your best life with both integrity and panache, considering the fact that one day you will die. I can't think of any subject more important to you or to me.

The Critical Struggle for Truth

As you read my guidelines for developing a coherent worldview, I urge you to listen for *the ring of truth.* As such, I am asking you to think counter to the damaging disregard for truth prevalent in our society today, which I call *truth decay.* The insights you encounter should ring a bell of recognition in your head (*Ah, yes, that's true... I had forgotten that.* Or, *Ah, that's right, I get it!*).

I use *that which corresponds to what really is* as the simple definition of truth. If I say, *Harrisburg is Pennsylvania's capitol,* and you know I'm right, you'll say, *That's true.* That's because my statement is not an opinion, a matter of taste, or something spoken in ignorance; it reports what is real—namely, that since 1810, Harrisburg has been Pennsylvania's official capital city. Of course, if you don't live in Pennsylvania, as I no longer do, this truth won't mean much to you. But because this book zeroes in on profound issues regarding life and death, truth is of utmost importance here. Only the truth will do.

People cite Ernest Hemingway as saying that searchers for truth need *gold-plated, built-in, shockproof crap detectors.* When I first heard this phrase, I envisioned scanners or invisible antennae sticking out of our skulls, ever sifting input for shreds of truth through all the TV commercials, junk mail, political spin, propaganda, disinformation, spam, manipulated statistics, public relations blather, and counterfeit claims that bombard us every day. I immediately thought to myself: *Hemingway is saying we need detectors to protect ourselves from outside onslaughts of untruth.* And God knows we need them. But then something more disturbing came to mind: We need these detectors to help us cut through all the deeply embedded crap or untruths we've let go unchallenged in our own understandings about living and dying.

Crap detector or no, rooting the falsehoods out of your worldview can be difficult. When you were a child, your parents and other authorities drummed into your head a lot of good and bad ideas they themselves had inherited and probably took for granted. Among other unworthy notions, they may have given you the impression that dying is a subject too threatening and depressing to think or talk about. If they did, whether or not they're still alive, to read and think about your death may make you feel as if you are disappointing them or even betraying them.

Of course, early on you may have challenged your parents' ideas and put your own worldview together piecemeal, the way a seamstress goes about making a patchwork quilt. But now, because you are so close to it and have so much invested in it, you may not be able to see that it might contain contradictions or untruths. More to the point, because every day, mainly through the sciences, we are grasping truer understandings of reality, no matter how you have come to your ideas about living and dying, your worldview may not pass the two tests for truth: (1) internal consistency, and (2) external correspondence to what we know is real today.

Further, you may have trouble picking out truth from falsehood because you live in a long wake of conflicting religious and philosophical traditions, each of which claims to hold *the* truth about what is ultimately real. In some way, at least some of them may have fortified or undermined your way of thinking. In addition, to bewilder you further, recent scientific developments have challenged many of the assumptions and conclusions of traditional philosophies and religions.

In a related problem, the simplistic figures in the fairy tales, religious stories, and pop culture you were exposed to as a child may continue to distort your grasp of reality. You heard about Santa Claus, the devil, the stork, the tooth fairy, the Easter bunny, the man upstairs, the boogeyman, and the grim reaper, whom I mention in my title. You've discarded most of these figures. But if you are typical, the *grim reaper* still lives in your mind, and he is a thief who can rob you of a shot at your best possible life. The time is past due for you to get rid of him, to *kill* him dead, and to put truth in his place. In part two, I will explain what the grim reaper stands for, why it is important to do away with him, and what it takes.

It's hard for all of us to know what to believe today, but I assume you think remaining open to truth is worthwhile and, while you may be willing to learn and change, you don't want to be among those who have given up what they used to believe, and, rather than believing nothing, will believe anything.

Sorting truth from falsehood will be even harder if you are dogged by chemical imbalance, a debilitating addiction, serious physical illness, or a negative view of yourself and life. And whether your struggles are big or small, to change your way of looking at reality can be scary as well as difficult. It's been that way for me at times, and I don't think I'm alone.

I've been stressing the notion that for you to be authentic, the insights and perspectives in your worldview must correspond to the truth. But cognitive coherence in your brain is not the only kind of truth important to pursue and claim. Another kind is truth that you live; it's a matter of *being* the truth. We call it *integrity,* which is the wholeness you experience when you live according to what you hold to be true. Integrity first requires you to be honest with yourself and remain open to who you are, no matter how hard it is to face.You experience integrity when you express not only the humanity you share with other humans and your uniqueness as a person but also what it means to be authentically human.

Unfortunately, most of us adults have sabotaged our best efforts to know this second kind of truth. When we were teens, we fought to discover who we were and said it was important for us to be true to ourselves. That was good for us. At the same time, because dying affronted our dignity and our sense of well being, we tried hard not to think about it and lived as if we never would die, though we knew we would. Under the control of this self-deception, we learned to put on false social faces so that others would think we were *truly together,* even though we weren't. All the while, those *others* were also wearing masks; and even though we knew they were as unhinged as we were, we let them fool us. In other words, we fooled ourselves. To our own detriment we still spend too much time protecting our facades or putting up *fronts,* trying to be perfect, not living in reality, and wasting energy we could give to being real and living our best possible lives. I am suggesting with this book that it's time to stop faking it and to cope more honestly with both life and the certainty of death.

Fortunately, the best in you is on your side. Despite Lily Tomlin's idea that *reality is the leading cause of stress for those in contact with it,* your true self wants you to live in the real world with authenticity. For you to demonstrate such integrity, you must embrace and live by understandings based on evidence and reason, rather than on mindless tradition, hearsay, wishful thinking, simpleminded superstitions, escapist fantasies, or any *blind* faith you brought from childhood or just grabbed on to last week.

If you can come to reasonable terms with this requirement and with the matters I discuss in the pages that follow, you can make immediate progress toward being true to yourself, killing the grim reaper, and living your best possible life. And fortunately, as with every worthy endeavor, in the pursuit of truth and the true self, joy comes not only with reaching your final destination but in the journey itself.

The information you will find in this book will serve your journey as an engine and a GPS, generating in you the freedom that comes with the combination of inner power and direction. As a result, you'll be able to better manage your routine days and cope with the curves, roadblocks, and painful surprises the world throws at you. And as you increasingly live by these truths, you will feel better about where you're going with your life and how you're getting there.

When you finish this book, you will feel more alive than ever before.

Heaven Without Death

Heaven without death:
Much desired;
With a proper frame of mind
Can be acquired.

To have more, want less, no platitude,
Can be achieved with the right attitude.
To suppress your needs;
Control your deeds.

Waking fresh from slumber deep,
Watching the morning sun creep
Over the flaming mountain crest,
Prepared to live each day at its best.

I have dealt with adversity
Survived the Great Depression and poverty.
Post war trauma from the good war we were told
Brought pain, darkness, suffering, and cold.

No blinkering my eyes to avoid seeing.
Rising to each challenge courageously,
Not letting life slip by vicariously,
Taking delight in overcoming each plight.

For heaven on earth
There will be no dearth.
I now discover the ability
For internal peace, love, and tranquility.
With my new voice, there is no other choice.

Ben Slomoff   June 2011

When you were born, you cried and the world rejoiced. Live your life in such a way so that when you die, the world cries and you rejoice.

Cherokee proverb

It's the one who won't be taken who cannot seem to give, And the soul, afraid of dying, that never learns to live.

The Rose

Teach us to number our days that we may get a heart of wisdom.

Psalm 90

PART ONE:

GENERATE A GOOD LIFE

A Magnificent Obligation

You starred on this promising occasion. Yet though you know the year, month, and day it happened, you remember nothing about it. Your mother—who also stars, bless her heart—forces you painfully from her uterus. A stranger holds you upside down by your ankles and slaps your bottom. You awake and cough up fluid you had swallowed while swimming in your prenatal habitat. You cry furiously. And we know for certain you do one other thing: You gasp for air and begin to breathe.

You still breathe. Whether you're asleep or awake, twenty times per minute and ten million times each year you draw breath to oxygenate the blood pumping from your heart to your lungs. This blood flows from your lungs back through your heart and into your sixty thousand miles of blood vessels, nourishing every part of you, including your large Homo sapiens brain. Sparked by revitalized blood, the lowest part of your reptilian brain stem, the medulla oblongata, relentlessly signals your respiratory system to keep breathing. It's happening as you read this sentence.

But to live your best life calls for more than taking one breath after another. It longs for, as someone has said, *moments that take your breath away*. It requires you to express fully your personality, to mature and to control as much of your own destiny as humanly possible, to follow thoughtfully your dreams and to live the potential that defines your true self. It asks you to nurture attitudes, perspectives, and actions that take time and focus to develop. It boils down to making sure you get on board and *love what makes the ride worthwhile*.

1

Renowned psychologist Abraham Maslow said, *If you deliberately plan to be less than you are capable of being, then I warn you that you will be deeply unhappy for the rest of your life.* Okay, some folks give up trying to be their best. Others get distracted by basic survival needs or by guilty pleasures. But does anyone *plan* not to live up to his or her full humanity? I don't think so. I think Maslow means that if you meander through your days in a daze, you will miss the joy of a life worthy of your dignity. But let me give his thought a positive twist: *If you give your best life your best shot, you will enrich the rest of your days.*

So you owe it to yourself to achieve your best life. You, alone, are responsible for your self, your life is primarily your experience of your self, and you are stuck with your self and your life until the day you die. Taking care of your self is your *magnificent obligation.*

You also owe your best life to those close to you, because it will enrich *them.* And if the seemingly selfless thought of enriching others doesn't grab you, get it into your brain that the *giving paradox* stands as a cycle of mutual benefit—when you live a life that enriches others, their responses in turn will enrich you in ways you owe it to yourself to experience.

The obligation to live your best life also comes from geography. Most people on this planet find life stacked against them, but in this country, your odds for living your best life and attaining *inner riches* are extraordinary. Our secular democracy, the healthy aspects of the Hebrew-Christian worldview, and the insights of science, including positive psychology, shape and inform the American consciousness today and pave the way for you to grasp spiritual riches that are as natural as breathing.

You also owe it to the universe to live your best possible life. It, or God if you will, dropped life into your lap as a gracious gift. You neither invented yourself nor did anything to deserve being born. In a sense, your life is on loan to you to nourish, help develop, and enjoy. And you are fortunate to exist, for the odds against your birth were greater than those of winning your state lottery…even if you bought a ticket.

Here's how good friend Eric Anschutz sees it. In his unpublished memoir, *October Song*, he takes from Annie Dillard's *For the Time Being* that there are 8.4 million possible mixes of maternal and paternal genes with any set of parents. He ruminates on the notion that, of all the possible persons that might have come from your parents' sexual union, *the one person who is uniquely you was born.* The 8,399,999 others who might have been conceived were not. They lost. You ended up with the prize, so to speak. And Anschutz doesn't like winners who are whiners:

> *How dare we complain about our lot in life, when the very fact that we are alive at all, against such staggering odds, is of such cosmic relevance? How dare we see ourselves as pedestrian, when our very existence results from the confluence of such unlikely events? … What we owe to life is to live it fully, to enjoy it, to smile and relax and enthuse about birds, and bees, and flowers, and clouds, and sunshine, and snow and sparkling waters, and (perhaps above all) one another.*

I figure the odds are much greater than 8.4 million-to-one against your being here. How likely was it that your biological parents would meet in the first place? What was the chance they would mate in that precise nanosecond about nine months before you were born? And think of this: Your mother took into herself some 300 million frantic, microscopic sperm. Only one single sperm cell, one with its twenty-three chromosomes and its particular genetic code, made its way to fertilize one of her eggs, an egg with its own particular twenty-three chromosomes and DNA. From that awesome combination, you were born, and other *potential* persons were cut off at the pass and denied life.

Here is something else to keep in mind: You won't harm yourself if you don't remember to breathe. Your brain will instruct your lungs to continue to draw oxygen for you, as it does when you sleep. But if you forget to come to terms with what your best life requires, or if you spend your days in an unthinking fog, you will subvert your noblest dreams and risk never becoming a real person. *The one thing you must not forget to do is to live your best possible life.*

3

Perhaps you've been trying to live that life all along, but you generally feel lost and sense that you have made little progress. The pages that follow offer perspectives that will help you approach living and dying creatively and constructively. The information and insights you'll find here can help you make a major difference in your life for the rest of your days.

In part one, I identify ten steps to clarify, expand, and strengthen your way of dealing with life. They will no doubt require you to change how you look at life and how you live. Along with healthy approaches to death (discussed in part two), they will give you a great shot at living robustly, even heroically, while touching this world with your positive contributions and helping you complete a worthwhile life.

In urging you to stretch your mind and make needed changes, I realize I may be pressing you to go against the very life you've been building and protecting since the day you were born. But it's a fair bet you've come this far with me because life isn't working very well and you want it to make it right. I encourage you to commit to taking any of the ten steps you think will help generate your best life.

You don't need to take all ten steps immediately, but as you read, I urge you to take right away those that come rather easily. It may be that you have already taken some of these steps, and what you read here may simply help you understand them better and reinforce their importance. You also don't need to take the ten in order, although reading them in order is a good idea, because from time to time I refer back to previous steps.

Some steps will no doubt require time and hard thinking to work through. When it comes to personal change, we are dealing with genes, temperaments, personalities, psychological and emotional conditioning, habits, and our individual histories. In addition, human development is dynamic and often uneven. Of course, the more diligently you work on taking the more difficult steps, the sooner you'll make genuine progress and the less risk you'll have of leaving behind *an unlived life* when you die.

Ten Critical Steps

Step One. Integrate Three Basic Models for the Human Journey

East and West have had their own models to describe human experience from birth to death. These models compete with each other and actually serve to divide East from West. Throughout history, they've given their adherents ways to understand and direct their lives, but they've also narrowed and limited their vision. We'll look at the two, and then review a dominant third model, one that arose mainly in the West in the twentieth century, and we'll talk about what to do with all three of them.

In the West, our standard model is a measurable line. It represents a journey with a starting point (birth, infancy, childhood), a middle trail (adolescence, young- and middle-age adulthood), and a final path leading to our destination (older adulthood and death). Life runs like a train from Station A, where we were born, to Station Z, where we die. Along the way, we encounter tunnels, curves, passages, starts and stops, roadblocks, bridges, open road, scenery, fellow travelers, and varied experiences that make our trip what it is. Despite twists and turns, we can symbolize this model with a horizontal line.

If we shift focus from our individual selves to the several millennium-long, linear trek of humanity, we encounter dramatic stories of families, tribes, nations, continents, genders, and races. The plots of our individual lives are written within and engulfed by such huge stories as the fate of our nation and of the Earth itself; we are all taking part in several dramas at once.

In *As You Like It*, Act 2, scene 7, Shakespeare has Jacques tell us, *All the world's a stage, and all the men and women merely players* .... Merely players, perhaps, but within history's compelling dramas, we not only act but we also write and direct our own subplots. We do this as we play collaborative roles with family, friends, and coworkers; struggle with unexpected dialogue; duel antagonists; and try to turn any tragedy into comedy. The most mundane steps we take have consequences that can catapult or stifle or even bring down the

5

curtain on the subplots we devise. Yet most of us make our way through the sequential scenes and acts of our lives, experiencing first-hand the tensions inherent in true drama, and head as best we can toward the inevitable but unpredictable final act of our life.

Each individual's drama is unique. At the same time, we identify with one another as a result of our common humanity, our intimate and functional associations, and the similar life passages we share. In our first three years, we get to know a bit of ourselves and our family, and begin to learn what's expected of us. We start to talk and walk, move from milk to pabulum to solid food, and hope to change from diapers to the potty. For most of us, not much happens that is exciting, but psychologists tell us these early years affect us even as adults, even though we remember next to nothing about them.

From preschool to about twelve years of age, we explore our bodies more seriously and our social situations become more complicated. Some of us recall from this period a special birthday, early sexual awakenings, favorite teachers and friends, a *crush* or early love, our most guilt-ridden and scariest moments, though most of our memories are fuzzy and random. Even so, we're told that these experiences, as do those we've forgotten from our first few years, continue to influence us today.

During puberty, or our teen years, we awkwardly express our new sexual vitality, wrestle with difficult moral dilemmas, and pass from dependence on our parents to independence. Most of us learn to protect ourselves, set priorities, establish routines, cultivate friendships, and take our first stab at discovering our interests and talents, even as greater exposure to the culture around us presses us to develop a broader view of the world.

After finishing our formal education, we try to find satisfying work while competing with others in a tough world. We remember experiences that were powerfully sexual, that gave us emotional highs or lows, that confused or threatened us, and that changed our views of the world and of ourselves.

In the next several decades, most of us build careers, try marriage, become parents, form households, and attempt to make a living. We do a lot of fantasizing about sex and love and hopefully learn to be better at both. We engage in various leisure activities and may volunteer in our communities. In these middle years, many of us suffer emotional blows, identity crises, and changes associated with maturity. We also spend a good deal of time trying to work out kinks in our most important relationships.

In our later years, our physical processes slow even as we keep busy with well-established routines. We may reflect a bit less on sex and focus more on retirement, health, and grandchildren. If we make it to retirement, we're even more aware of declining energy and perhaps of *having lived a life*. We feel a rise and a fall of *aliveness* from the early years through middle age into our later years. This pattern suggests an arc, rather than a straight line, as a model for the linear life.

Under this Western model, to live your best possible life you must do what you can to write your own story from your early adult years through a reasonably projected life span. As you write, however, you must pay attention to the large dramas of your community, your country, and the world. They, on the on the hand, have the power to overwhelm or immobilize you, and on the other, to help you make your contributions—no matter how insignificant—to the higher and larger good. If you can creatively connect with them, life will gain depth, you'll see yourself as a valuable member of the human race, and you'll rightly feel good about yourself.

The second model for human life comes from Eastern philosophy. While Eastern sages acknowledge a linear dimension to our experience, they traditionally describe life as *cyclical* and use a circle or spiral as its symbol. They look at life as a series of beginnings, endings, and new beginnings, and emphasize the cycle of birth, life, death, and reincarnation. To portray the move from childhood dependence to adolescent independence and adult interdependence, and then, in old age, back to childlike dependence, they use a full-circle image. A dark and light interactive circle represents the complementary yet opposing male and female forces of yin and yang that Eastern philosophers believe hold human life in balance.

This Eastern view depends on the lunar calendar, and encourages us to move in harmony with the rhythms and movements of the major bodies in our solar system. The cyclical pattern is represented by the following:

- The circling of the sun by the Earth (the annual three-hundred-and-sixty-five-day cycle, with its seasons and cyclical weather patterns);

- The orbiting of the moon around the Earth (the monthly calendar echoed in the menstrual cycle);

- The quarter-moon cycle in the lunar month (the seven-day week);

- The rotation of the Earth on its axis (twenty-four hours, or a day and night).

The Chinese calendar also blends symbols from astrology and nature that represent twelve-year cycles. Achieving five of them by the age of sixty is considered special and is one of the reasons Asians revere the elderly. This system is not a fad; the Chinese have been honoring sixty-year cycles since the twenty-seventh century BC. With the large influx of Asians into North America in past fifty years, many Americans, especially on the West Coast, have become at least somewhat familiar with their cyclical model of looking at life.

When things aren't going well, knowing that morning follows night can allow you the courage to say, *This too will change, I will try again tomorrow.* According to Eastern wisdom, no matter where you live, if you tune your activity to the rhythm of rejuvenating natural cycles, you can claim any number of new beginnings and be energized to live your best possible life.

The third model, I call *episodic*. Whether you have been reared on the linear or the cyclical model, life is full of random interruptions, surprising stops and starts, and emergencies that constantly redirect and reshape your existence. This model sees life not as a straight, unbroken line from the past through the present to the future, but as ongoing, unpredictable interruptions that stop you dead in your tracks one moment and take you all over the map the next. The only constant in this model is discontinuity. The symbol for an episodic view of live is a broken line—straight, arced, or circular.

Interruptions can be seen primarily as disturbances or opportunities. You may experience them as both. Some you will have control over; other you won't. Some merely may disrupt the subplots with which you are living comfortably, and be annoying. Others may be big enough to throw you off track, push you to the sidelines or face you with detours, causing you to stop and back up, or even temporarily halt your journey. Major subplot disruptions such as the arrival of your first child, the loss of a job, divorce, a major health setback, or the death of someone close to you, can force you to radically change your plans and goals. They may turn you back in your linear journey or full circle in any cyclical pattern you've been following. They can make your dreams fade and be terribly painful and debilitating.

Most proactive Americans expect to develop a positive plot for their linear lives, but few of us reach old age without our plots being rewritten, at least to some degree. All of us have lived with mega episodes, such as 9/11 and Hurricane Katrina, that without warning, disrupt the peace not only of national life but also of our personal lives, even when they don't directly impact us. Such events can strike us as out of line, for they fail to fit with what we've hoped for and how we think life and our dreams should unfold. And when we try to make sense of them, they may strike us as meaningless except for any meaning we give them.

Modern European films have tended to portray real life as painfully episodic and disconnected. Seemingly related events turn out to be totally unconnected; and the stories often end unhappily. We may not like it, but discontinuity and chaos in nature, politics, finances, career plans, relationships, family life, and health define our life as much, if not more, than the plots we devise. Novelist Ivy Compton-Burnett notes, *Real life seems to have no plots. And as*

9

I think a plot desirable and almost necessary, I have this extra grudge against life. Some of us may feel this way, but most of us know it's foolish to think of life as only *happy trails* with an inevitable wonderful ending.

A central question for each of us concerns how to handle episodic interruptions so they contribute to our best possible life. Some people handle them well; others resent them and become defeated. Most of us have a mixed response. The point is that the more aware we are of the normality and the *predictability of unpredictable episodes,* the better we are able to handle them. If we can come to terms with the fact that *life is rife with interruptions* that disrupt our plans, it makes them more bearable and frees us to cope with change.

We have looked at three life models: linear, cyclical, and episodic. I argue that we sell ourselves short when we cling to the model we were given and dismiss the others as false or unnecessary. This reduces reality to our own small take on things. I propose that life is much too large, complex, and mysterious for one model, and that to live your best possible life you must find what is real and positive in each of these models. It shakes down to something like this:

- **You will do well to design your own linear journey to the degree that you can.** To know where you've been can help you discover who and where you are and what directions you need to take. This knowledge can help you maintain a high quality of life.

- **You will do well to stay close to natural, cyclical rhythms.** They can help you appreciate the repeated chances you have to rise above your mistakes and failures and start over, whether every year, every month, every week, or every morning.

- **You will do well to integrate interrupting episodes into your life.** You may benefit from emergencies, bumpy rides, and surprises, if you see them as natural to your experience, are ready for them, can roll with the punches, take them as opportunities when you can, and weave them into your life patterns.

To live our best possible life, we must abandon any narrow lens through which we've been looking at life and let all three of these models shape our worldview.

Step Two. Adopt a Positive View of Life That is Realistic

A man has twin sons—one is a seemingly incurable optimist, and the other an unrepentant pessimist. They drive their father crazy, and he's had enough. For their birthday, he gives them gifts he thinks might help cure their lopsidedness. He places the finest gold Rolex he can find in a small, beautiful box for the pessimist. For the optimist, he fills a plain brown bag with horse manure. When the pessimist opens the little box with his name on it, he laments, *Damn! I got a watch, and in a week it will probably be running slow.* The optimist opens his gift and exclaims, *Oh, boy! I got a pony, but he ran away.*

Most of us approach life with optimism or with pessimism, depending on our disposition, on how we were treated as children, and on the dominant worldview of the culture or subculture we grew up in. Both perspectives are hard to break or even modify, and neither leads to our best possible life. In this section, I'll explain why and describe a third way that puts us more in touch with reality and helps us achieve our goal.

Pessimism is viewing life negatively. Pessimistic people bow to Murphy's Law: *If something can go wrong, it will, and at the worst possible time.* They say *the glass of life is half empty (or perhaps mostly or fully empty).* Believing they've never had a full glass, or convinced that others must have drunk it dry, pessimists aren't hopeful about quenching their deepest thirsts. After a while, they may become cynical and view life as absurd and wretched.

People who obsess about the down side say *life is …one damned thing after another* (Frank Ward O'Malley); *…a series of inspired follies* (G. B. Shaw); *…a tale told by an idiot, full of sound and fury, signifying nothing* (Shakespeare); *…a bitch, and then you die! (anonymous, and quoted by scads of cynical pessimists).*

11

In a less serious vein, pessimist Rodney Dangerfield thinks life is not a bowl of cherries but *a bowl of pits*. Mel Brooks entitled his tongue-in-cheek film *Life Stinks!* Woody Allen thinks life is divided into *the horrible and miserable*. Our ability to laugh at our predicaments may offer much-needed salvation, but chronic pessimism can deter you from living your best life.

Today, random acts of violence, world terrorism, climate change, dysfunctional political, business and social systems, the control of our democracy by multinational corporations, crass telemarketing, and any number of technical breakdowns or your own personal ills may influence you to view life, at least at times, as *one damned thing after another*. Even at this moment, you may see your personal life as stalled, sidetracked and seemingly hopeless.

If you think about it, however, parts of your life, like parts of the universe and our current society, are good or promising. The odds are that you have not suffered abject poverty, plagues or untreated disease, unrelieved hunger, harsh political tyranny, or the relentless misery that has given people throughout history real reasons to view life pessimistically. When we compare our lot to that of others, we often see our situation more clearly and more realistically. The truth is that we who can read, think, and act on our own behalf stand among the relatively few on Earth who are in a position to help better themselves, their country, and the world.

By contrast, a second way people view life is through rose-colored lenses of gleeful optimism. Optimists can't help but see the glass as half full, and it's often full, or even running over. And they always seem to believe that the best is yet to come. They say things like *Life is...beautiful!* (screenwriter Roberto Benigni), or compare life to a merry-go-round and admit that it is *better than the alternative.* Pessimists as well as optimists tend to believe it is probably better to look at life positively rather than negatively. The philosopher, William James suggests that if you believe life is worth living, your belief will help create the fact. I think there is some truth in that, but it's not the whole truth, and while we can understand why pessimists envy optimists, optimism also has its limitations.

Most American optimists base their attitudes on Pollyannaish religious perspectives. Think of Norman Vincent Peale in the early twentieth century (the power of positive thinking); of the once prominent, pioneer televangelist Robert Schuller (possibility thinking); and today's ever-smiling media star Joel Osteen (the prosperity gospel). All three preachers instruct their followers to fill their minds with lovely thoughts, cultivate a never-give-up attitude, and keep a stiff upper lip with a fixed smile. They fortify their teachings with upbeat music, beautiful flowers, and affluence. They don't want followers to think about suffering, failure, poverty, necessary conflict, or death.

Optimism may help people see past their problems for the moment, but when things don't turn out as planned, optimists often feel betrayed, angry, guilty, and defeated. If that's not bad enough, they tend to miss the character-building lessons of hard times and the self-esteem rewards that come from working through tough situations. Like pessimism, optimism fails to respect both sides of the real world and stops us from living fully.

I propose a third view, one that is both positive *and* realistic. Believers of this philosophy see the glass as half empty *and* half full, often all at the same time. Sometimes it's overflowing and sometimes it's empty. This perspective grasps life's ups and downs, including the finality of dying. It won't let its believers deny life's darker side, but it also won't let them wallow in their hardships or allow them to set their own agendas or self-identify as pessimists. It asks people to see problems and difficult situations as sources of learning and transformation. This approach calls for living intentionally, not only *under* your circumstances but also *above* them, and to approaching negatives in such a way you try to turn them into positives.

You try to be right about everything. Isn't that so? If you are the classic pessimist, I suggest you use this to your advantage. You can become one who actively seeks positives in every experience. No matter how bad a situation or person might appear, say to yourself, *I don't like this, but it is what it is, and I am going to find a positive in it.* Your subconscious will take this commitment as an order and, wanting to do what is right, will do everything it can to transform your negative into a positive, your bad day into a good one.

13

People with this view often see life as a series of puzzles to solve, tests to pass, or challenges to meet. The challenges sometimes excite and sometimes discourage them. Either way, they believe that if the water of life is to fill their glass, they must fill it themselves. For them life is ...*difficult* (Scott Peck); ...*an advanced institution of learning* (Thomas Edison); ...*a tough proposition, and the first hundred years are the hardest* (Minzer); and ...*like a box of chocolates—you never know what you're gonna get* (from *Forrest Gump*).

A realistic and hopeful outlook asks you to see the context of your life as the mixed bag that it is. You may trust a universe that gives you flowers, butterflies, and rainbows, but you must not forget its weeds, poisonous insects, and killer earthquakes. It's important to remember that some people inflict atrocities on innocents, such as was the case on 9/11 and at the Columbine, Virginia Tech, and Tucson massacres, but it's equally critical to keep in mind there are noble, heroic, and philanthropic people. The world includes both good and evil; life is a mix of joy and sorrow; and we give our lives a vibrant rhythm when we dance back-and-forth between our potential and our limitations.

This view of life requires you to accept both your failures and your successes. When you will think of life as a merry-go-round, you will see both the risk of falling off and the chance to grab gold rings—it's a terrifying challenge and an exhilarating adventure all in one. If you adopt this view, it will help you define your life not only by your eventual death but also by the opportunity to live robustly for all the time you have left.

People who see life this way often have mixed feelings. When adherents are succeeding more than failing (or when good things come their way), they tend to view life as good and get out of bed most mornings able to—if not happy to—face the day. When they go to bed dwelling on the day's problems and defeats, they tend to have difficulty getting up to tackle what the next day demands. Whether more optimistic or more pessimistic, their successes and failures and what happens from one morning to the next may change both their outlook and their mood.

If you've always been either a pure pessimist or an undaunted optimist, like the twin sons discussed earlier, your narrow perspective may have such a grip on you that it will be hard to change. You may enjoy your way of approaching life too much and not want to give it up. It may provide excuses for your failures, and you don't want to lose those excuses. Most of us find it hard to break habits, even when we know they are self-defeating.

Sometimes change is easy once you get the picture. Simply seeing the three approaches we have discussed side by side may enable you to employ this third lens from now on. And if you have tended to be pessimistic, it will be easier and more satisfying once you commit to learn from negatives and change them into positives.

If looking at life in this third way is too hard for you, you don't have to make it a lifelong commitment. Get out your calendar. Try looking at life as both tragedy and comedy for a limited time, experimenting by taking whatever comes your way and getting *above the circumstances*. Begin by marking *G&B* (for good and bad) on each day in your calendar for the next week. Or put two simple faces on all of them, one with a smile and the other with a frown.

If you've been an optimist, when you check your calendar each morning it still will allow you to relish your successes and positive experiences. But you won't have to resort to denial when you fail or meet a negative experience, for you now know we all are flawed and negatives as well as positives exist in all our lives. If you've leaned toward pessimism, your calendar notes should remind you of life's positives, and a failure or mistake shouldn't push you back into negativism. No matter which attitude feels most natural to you, picking up this third lens can broaden, stabilize, and liberate you. You'll be better able to enjoy good times, take rough times more easily in stride, valuing their hard lessons, and you will develop a deeper sense of wholeness.

How do you answer the following four questions?

- Is it shortsighted to look only at the rosy side of life?

- Do you damage yourself if you only view life negatively?

- From day to day, does life vary from depressing to delightful?

- Can one's view of life be both positive and realistic?

My response to each of these questions is *yes*.

Step Three. Claim an Important Level of Freedom for Yourself

If you conduct a survey asking Americans what controls or directs the universe, human history, and their lives, some will say, *I am not sure*. We have no shortage of theories, however, and the vast majority of those who've given it any thought at all draw on one of four answers: 1) God, 2) evolution, 3) fate, and 4) themselves (at least with regard to their own lives). Some try to integrate elements from two or more answers, and some believe one thing with their heads and another with their hearts—sentiment and intellect often conflict.

I suggest that to live your best life, one question you must deal with is *how much control you have over your life and death*. To some degree, your answer to the broader question of *what, if anything, is in charge of the universe and your life* determines how you respond to this narrower question. Look with me at the four choices more closely.

First, many religious believers claim that an *intelligent power* predetermines all that is. They contend that in the distant past, an all-powerful deity, their loving creator God, made everything out of nothing. Since then, nothing has happened, is happening, or will happen, good or bad, without God determining it. These believers may sing, *He's got the whole world in his hands*, or they may shout, *God is great!*

16

They also say that humans are made in this deity's image, which means, among other things, that we all possess godlike freedom, creativity, and the ability to respond, or *response-ability*. The combination of our freedom and God's unlimited power poses two critical problems: One, the two notions appear to contradict each other. If God predetermines everything, then we don't have free will; if we have free will, God does not determine everything. To expose this contradiction, when asked if he believed in predestination or in free will, Jewish Nobel laureate Isaac Singer said, tongue in cheek: *We have to believe in free will; we've got no other choice.*

The second issue is, if God causes everything, then God must be the author of evil and suffering in the world. And if God is the mastermind behind tens of thousands of children dying of starvation and horrible diseases every day, how can God be called loving? To give the all-powerful, loving God a way out and make room for freedom and responsibility on our part, some theologians contend that everything happens not according to God's *predetermined plan,*but with God's *permission.* Let me see if I have this clear? It's not God's intention that children should die all too brief, painful, and meaningless lives... but God *permits* it? And that makes God loving? Anyway, since God is sovereign and you do have some ability to shape your life, people who think this way suggest that when you feel lost or threatened, *pray as if everything depends on God* and *work as if it depends on you.* You can make a difference.

Other believers hold to a different kind of God. Their God, they say, is not a separate, wholly other, sovereign being, or the *big guy in the sky,* but rather, in Paul Tillich's famous phrase, the *ground of all being,* or the life-defining *spiritual power of love.* This God, or genuine love, shows us what it takes to be ethical and genuinely human, but it cannot force us to those good ends. It is limited not only by natural law, the relentless but tediously slow march of evolution, human weakness and perversity but also by its very nature as genuine love.

The responsible freedom that this love nurtures, actually defines and helps us make sense of being adult humans. When we do what is constructive, healthy, and noble, when we go with the good, or God, or love, we enrich and dignify ourselves. When we do nothing in the face of evil, or when we fail to do what enhances life, we thwart the will of this God, demeaning and destroying ourselves. Though the heart of this God is broken when we act self-destructively, God can do nothing but continue to woo us toward wholeness. Such staggering patience and forgiveness, encourages us to grow up, to let go of past failures and to face the future corrected and with confidence. We'll probe the significance of genuine love a bit deeper in step ten.

A second answer to the question of what controls the universe is the scientific theory of evolution. It tells us that over billions of years, physical laws such as gravity and centripetal force, along with chemical and biological processes, have determined the nature, shape, and direction of everything that is. Because you and I are subject to these laws, we don't—or can't—break them; and if we try to, they break us. Through evolution, your magnificent brain developed enough to give you the amazing consciousness that enables you to read and find the meaning in this sentence.

The different sciences say we don't have very much freedom, if any. Biology dictates that genes, various chemicals and hormones determine personality, temperament, and behavior. The social sciences argue that geography, gender, race, religion, culture, and economic class define who we are and how we behave. The behavioral sciences tell us that in our formative years both good or bad parenting and traumas we experience, along with the compulsions they create, largely determine how we act and what we become.

These scientific views had little influence before the twentieth century. Adults were seen as morally free agents who, with the knowledge of commonly held standards of right and wrong, were seen as responsible for their character, their actions, and their own well-being. But for the past half century or so, scientific understanding, rooted in evolution, has been at the core of public school and higher education. As a consequence, most educated Americans today believe that genes, hormones, brain cell activity, birth order, parenting, childhood traumas, cravings for social acceptance, unconscious drives, and addictions limit our freedom and have a lot more to do with how we behave than does personal freedom.

This view has come to dominate child-rearing philosophies as well as our educational and criminal justice systems, so both children and adults today are often let off the hook for behaviors that in the past were considered immoral, unhealthy, and even criminal. In its most extreme form, this view says that if you received ill treatment from your parents as a child and exhibit no self-control over your actions, you ought not to be held responsible for your behavior. Critics refer to this as *the abuse excuse*.

A third possibility for what controls the universe is fate. Fate says that the laws of nature, chance, coincidence, fear, compulsive drives, and actions, plus strong social forces interact to produce unpredictable outcomes and determine what happens to you, how you behave, and who you become. If you believe in fate, you have concluded that many things happen randomly, often triggered by the acts of others, with no apparent rhyme or reason. Also, seemingly insignificant choices can impact your life in major ways. For example, you might take one of two possible roads home one night and become involved in (or just miss) a serious accident; or the airline might assign you a seat next to a total stranger who ends up becoming your husband. Such events can be seen as the workings of fate.

Believers in fate know choices have consequences, but they insist it's an illusion to believe that you have much to do with who you are and what your life is like. They see life mostly in terms of luck—pure luck, good luck, bad luck, dumb luck, and no luck at all. Aristotle said that luck (meaning good luck) is when the fellow next to you gets hit with the arrow. How often has your life turned on what appears to be good or bad luck?

Fatalists try to find meaning in happenings over which they have no control. They say, *It was meant to be simply because it happened*, or, *Whatever will be, will be* (you can't do anything about it). When they talk about their careers, their life partners, what their general lot in life becomes, and how, where, and when they die, they speak of *destiny*. This dramatic term implies that your life is primarily determined by powers other than yourself, leaving you with little if any control over your life.

To see things this way robs you of a sense of freedom, which we like to think is a distinctive mark of the human animal. And that theft is dehumanizing—you cannot feel the dignity of an intelligent, creative, free being when your life is totally at the mercy of indifferent forces. And nothing does more to demean your humanity than for you to charge your bad decisions to some other power, rather than take responsibility for your life.

If your life has been twisted in ways you don't understand and couldn't control if you wanted to, you may chalk it up to providence (*God loves me; God loves me not*), to evolution (*I'm at the mercy of the great process that can't show mercy*), or to fate (*Whatever will be will be*). You also may see two or more of these forces intermixing, at least to some degree, or you may not be able to distinguish between them. Evolution and fate, in contrast to the providence of theistic religions, are impersonal and deterministic. Neither can be said to have *intention* or to *care* about your welfare, as can a freedom-granting, loving God. But evolution, fate, and Western theism all say that a power greater than us determines what happens to us and how we live.

A fourth view contends we are self-made by the strength of our will and the choices we make. Advocates have heard of God, evolution, and fate, but they look at human potential and freedom very differently. They may concede that we have no control over when, where, or to whom we are born, but they reject the notion we are scripted by nature, society, or any other power to the point that we are not responsible for our lives. They downplay our weaknesses, addictions, and pathologies and highlight our ability to choose. They say that luck is not altogether accidental or blind, but that to a large degree we make our own luck and determine our own destiny.

This position finds extreme expression in the poem *Invictus* by William Ernest Henley, who wrote, in spite of the great obstacles he faced in his own life, *I am the master of my fate; I am the captain of my soul.* I find Henley's acceptance of responsibility admirable, and such self-reliance can produce good things in our lives. But if we are looking for truth here, his indifference to, if not rejection of, other powers that determine what we are and how we behave loses touch with reality And it's important to keep in mind that sooner or later the captain will go down with the ship, which is a reality we'll get to later on

Here, it seems to me, is the problem we all face: Not providence, nor evolution, nor fate, nor rugged individualism can adequately answer the question of *who or what is in charge of the universe and our lives*. We are left to struggle with the following questions:

- Can any one of these views explain all I experience and need?

- Must I see these four options as mutually exclusive?

- Do I know enough to deny the realities of any of these views?

My answer to each of these questions is no. But the central one remains: To what degree does *response-ability* define you and me? I realize this is a question we may never be able to answer to everyone's satisfaction, but I operate on the basis of this important conviction: *No matter what you believe, you and I have enough freedom to make life better for the world around us, for those we love, and for ourselves.*

We know we can't do everything, but we can do *something*. And while your faith in God, evolution, or fate may take you to a crossroads, set up a roadblock, or point you in a new direction, *it is up to you to take it from there.* To forget this principle may invalidate your humanity and leave you unduly stalled and burdened. At the least, you will miss the opportunity to help make this world better by creating your own best life.

At the same time, believing in providence, evolution or fate requires you to accept a power greater than yourself may take you through tough times you won't like and may not understand. If your faith is in God (*Why me?*). To live your best life, you must face challenges with courage and integrity, finding the good in them when possible, making the most of them and adding depth to your *character.* I think we must grant that believers in God have tended to roll with the punches and make the most of difficulties (*It must be God's will*), but almost everyone can see that, if life is handed to us on a silver platter or we take a charmed life for granted, we have little chance of developing inner strength and maturity.

While most of us want what we want when we want it, the Dalai Lama encourages us to see that when we don't get what we want, it may be *a wonderful stroke of good luck*. The nonreligious Broadway director and producer Hal Prince, a self-professed fatalist, endured many hard knocks early in his life, and at the time they occurred he hated them. But as an adult he came to believe the burdens fate had placed on him taught him important lessons and changed him for the better. He is quoted as saying, *Sometimes bad luck is the best luck*.

Life's surprises and heavy loads can overwhelm or kill us, so to live our best life it's smart to call on available resources: family and friends; laws and social systems; the wisdom of the ages; the knowledge, stamina and inner strength gained from experience; and the myriad spiritual powers that wise people tap into to increase their freedom and self-control. For example, to cope with addiction, pain, anxiety, and weakness, many people recite the Serenity Prayer, originally penned by theologian Reinhold Niebuhr: *God, give us the grace to accept with serenity the things that cannot be changed, the courage to change the things that should be changed, and the wisdom to distinguish the one from the other.*

I suggest that a narrow, one-sided approach to the central human question of personal freedom limits your control over both your life and your death and betrays your best interests. So the question remains: Will you broaden your view of the powers that control your life to include yourself and then exercise responsible freedom to make the most of your living and dying?

Step Four. Choose Life Purposes That Ennoble and Empower You

It's been said that *the supreme purpose of life is to live with supreme purpose.* Sadly, the three life purposes most Americans adopt strike me as shallow, ignoble, and self-defeating:

1. **Gobble up all you can for yourself:** This materialistic purpose assumes that the one with the most, latest, and biggest toys wins. It's not only self-defeating if you are a loser, but it's also a losing formula in itself, because it sets you against everybody else, including those you need to complete your life, leaving you alienated and empty. Actually, it betrays you by focusing on what you want rather than what you need. It also prompts you to excess, and we know that excess destroys us—too much of even a good thing is...too much . In the end, it will identify you simply as a sad and self-absorbed consumer.

2. **Get others to like you:** The social *disease to please* will relentlessly drive you to do what you think others want you to do. It's a psychological sickness in contrast to doing what you know is right and what is good for others and yourself. It's a pathetic excuse for living that will compel you at every moment to win friends, rather than simply to be friendly. And unlike choosing to serve others, trying to please them robs you of the joy that comes with taking responsibility for your life, managing it well, and living your best life.

3. **Get to heaven when you die:** This religious formula diverts your attention and energies away from living fully and from helping make this world better. In a baseball metaphor, it compares your life here and now to spring training, or the exhibition season, and makes an afterlife the season that counts. In an endless focus on everlasting life, it promotes an extreme preoccupation with yourself. Toward the end of the book we'll look at issues related to belief in the afterlife.

These popular life purposes invalidate any meaning we can assign to being mature and authentic. They betray you by arresting your development, blocking your freedom, and stopping you from achieving dignity as a human being. So I encourage you to read again the three paragraphs and swear off on these shallow life purposes, one by one. Then, stay with me as

I discuss how you can jump-start your pursuit of purposes worthy of your humanity.

One thing strikes me as undeniably central to human purpose and important for us to understand: You and I are meant to grow up. We are to develop in every way—physically, emotionally, intellectually, socially, morally, and spiritually. Our central task is to fully live out our nature. If you do that, you can create your best possible life. But personal growth doesn't happen automatically. We must do our part by making responsible choices and efforts. As Chili Davis points out, *Growing old is mandatory; growing up is optional.*

Worthy purposes help you grow. They nourish your spirit, enlarge your positive effect on others, and set you up to live your best possible life. If your development has been seriously stunted, you will be constantly acting counterproductively, negatively affecting yourself and others, and failing to esteem yourself. If this describes you, it may be because you have been pursuing shallow purposes unworthy of your humanity (and haven't we all met thirty-year-old children and sixty-year-old adolescents?).

You can't change how you've lived up to now, but to enrich your life immediately, you can start giving time and energy to the following life purposes (not in order of importance or mutually exclusive):

1. **Follow your passion and express your gifts in practical ways that contribute to the common good.**

2. **Ground, integrate, balance, and liberate yourself with a worldview shaped by truth so you can be your best self, fulfill your chosen roles, and cultivate positive relationships.**

3. **Develop your capacity to express compassion so you deepen your relationships and help alleviate human suffering.**

4. **Add to the beauty and goodness that enriches us all by sharing what you've learned about being authentically human.**

5. **Embrace difficult adventures and challenges that will help you develop wisdom and character.**

6. **Throw yourself into helping renew your country and protect the environment for future generations.**

7. **Expand your knowledge of what the world must do to survive by contributing to justice, peace and a sustainable future.**

When you choose from such worthy purposes, you elevate your status from primate to true person. Experience tells us that the opportunity to work hard at things that are worth doing is one of the greatest rewards of life. If you have trouble grasping this, let me suggest that you ask yourself,

By my life, how do I show what I'm living for?

Where do I now, and where will I put my energy, money, and time?

To what ends can I best devote myself for the rest of my life?

Before I die, what can I do to feel genuinely good about myself?

For what righteous cause am I willing to suffer and die, and why?

If you have trouble trying to answer these questions, go back to the three shallow and the seven worthwhile life purposes I've just identified. Cross out those you disavow and those that won't work for you. Let stand, and list in priority order, those that suit your particular gifts and interests, and underline any you are willing to adopt and work on.

To pursue your purposes, you will need to determine how to best expend your time and energy toward them, even as you cut out those things that are a drag on your vitality. Goethe tells us things that matter most must never be at the mercy of things that matter the least. In other words, for your own sake, set priorities and don't let mundane trivialities get in the way.

If your everyday work channels your *passion*, and you *help lift the world forward* as well as earn income, at a vocational level you already may feel near to your best possible life. If so, count yourself fortunate. If your work puts a roof over your head, bread on the table, and offers some of the popular amenities, but the labor itself delivers little meaning and satisfaction to your life, then you may have to make a job change or even switch careers in order to achieve your best life.

If a new job or a different vocation are out of the question right now, you can make your life matter more by how you spend your leisure hours. Once you identify your passion and acknowledge your skills, you may want to find community projects through which to express them. It's a matter of committing your heart and mind to responsible and rewarding service.

You can talk to friends who have taken on worthwhile projects. You also might check with a local school, homeless shelter, arts center, museum, or your faith community, if you have one. If you don't know an organization that would welcome your time and gifts, talk with friends, go online or dig into the Yellow Pages to find one that will.

You might pose these kinds of questions to yourself: Can you identify an injustice that riles you, but you don't know what to do about it? Is an entity in government treating the poor shabbily but it seems too big an injustice for you to deal with? Are you aware of a corporation that exploits its employees, some segment of our society, or the poor at home or abroad?

Perhaps you have been working with others to help stop an injustice and have been discouraged. Naturally you want to right the wrong. At the same time, in the end it's as important that you remain *faithful* to justice as it is that you *succeed*. It's a matter of doing and being the truth, whether you win or not. Such living with integrity offers its own internal rewards.

At the same time, I encourage you to beware of *do-goodism*—that is, doing something for how good it makes you feel whether or not your service really provides what is needed. Sadly, those with strengths, resources and good intentions, too often patronize the oppressed and do more harm than good.

Also, just because an organization commits to a worthy cause does not mean it is effective or offers a satisfying experience. Poor organization, bad policies and procedures, sloppy communication, and people with weak egos can ruin the best of possible experiences. No group, no well-meaning person, including you, is perfect. You will do well to check out a group's mission statement and bylaws, if it has such things (if it doesn't, be wary, or if you're experienced with such things, you might help it develop them). If you can't discern the group's value and effectiveness immediately, make it clear you are in it on a trial basis. Ask leaders and followers in the group what they think are its strengths and weaknesses. If the weaknesses dominate, explain to the leadership why you are going to volunteer elsewhere. And, if after a somewhat diligent search, you don't find anything, or your health won't let you be active, settle for giving respectful love to everyone you meet and wait for a project to emerge. You also could e-mail your elected representative about an issue you are passionate about or write cards to political prisoners through Amnesty International (more on this organization later).

If you have the security of solid work and a decent home, it's critical to realize that you don't have to settle for mediocrity, or for limits others put on you. I'm not saying you can do anything you want; few among us can. But you can awaken your imagination by doing something that will use your gifts, serve a worthy purpose, enrich your spirit, and make you proud of what you're living for. Someone sent me these words by a poet whose name I've been unable to find:

> *All that you dreamed but didn't dare to do,*
> *all that you hoped but did not will,*
> *all the faith that you claimed but did not have—*
> *these slumber lightly,*
> *waiting to be awakened.*

Many people have awakened.

I think of Hal Taussig, a college mate of mine and a champion wrestler. After graduation, he returned to the family business of cattle ranching and soon went broke. Fortunately, he saw opportunity in his loss. Somewhere along the line he soured on the work ethic that tells us to make our way up and leave everyone else behind. He took a sabbatical to tour Europe in a Volkswagen, and it inspired an idea—a travel agency that will enable tourists to get to know a town intimately by staying at least two weeks in a rented cottage, apartment, or farmhouse. With a five-thousand-dollar loan from a friend, Taussig launched Untours in 1975. In the early 1980s, he was making more money from the operation than he needed and decided to live simply by accepting twenty thousand dollars a year for his basic expenses.

After sharing excess profits with his customers and employees, he set up the Untours Foundation, which provides low-interest loans to create jobs, build low-income housing, and support fair-trade products. Since the early 1990s, such loans have ranged from six thousand dollars to two hundred and fifty thousand dollars. Some fifty organizations and individuals have benefited from Untours seed money. Hal Taussig, who's given away millions, believes the widening gap between the rich and poor is not sustainable. He says that Untours is his way of finding meaning and joy in life.

I met Ellen Kalm in the 1970s. At thirteen, in a Nazi death camp, she vowed not to waste her life if she survived. As a child she discovered that she had a pleasant voice and learned to play the piano. When I met her, she was a musical therapist for Children's Hospital in Oakland, California. When I asked what a musical therapist does, she said, *I teach dying children to sing.* For forty years, she's brought joy to children with cystic fibrosis, congenital birth defects, and terminal cancer. As I write, she volunteers at an end-of-life residential facility for children. Do you think that Ellen, at the age of eighty, has a problem determining whether she's lived her best possible life?

There are millions of rich life stories like those of Hal Taussig and Ellen Kalm. Likewise, there are untold numbers of similar causes that beg for attention. Do you really want to live your best possible life? Identify what time you can offer and the skills you might hone to meet one of those needs. In other words, start gathering ideas to write your own wonderful story.

In the end, only you can decide what you believe and do about pursuing worthy purposes for your life. Whether or not you make your life more worthwhile, at the end of the day the only actions to judge are your own. How others live their lives is up to them. A nonsmoker once said to his smoker friend, *Think of the castles you could build with all that money you spend on cigarettes.* The smoker replied, *So where are your castles?*

That's a question we all might ask of ourselves.

Step Five. Engage Life with Both Passion and Good Sense

You can't drop out of the world and live your best life. At some level, you must be a passionate participant. You are a vital member of the human community. Life is to be lived with vibrant spirit, connections to others, and the responsibility to honor every opportunity for joy in the world. The knowledgeable W. H. Auden said that he didn't know anything except what we all know, that—*if there when Grace dances, I should dance.* At the same time, passion can be costly. It can shake up your priorities, change your life's direction, and propel you into the powerful vortexes of the human drama, which, of course, produce tragedy as well as comedy.

Some great thinkers advocate full-tilt passion with work. English playwright George Bernard Shaw said, *I want to be thoroughly used up when I die, for the harder I work the more I live. I rejoice in life for its own sake.* When he died at age ninety-four, after an unusually productive life, he was, indeed, used up.

Famed writer, Hunter S. Thompson is quoted widely as saying something like this (there are myriad versions): *Life should not be a journey to the grave with the intention of arriving in a beautiful and well preserved body, but rather to skid in broadside in a cloud of smoke, chocolate in one hand, martini in the other, thoroughly used up, totally worn out, and loudly proclaiming, "Wow! What a ride!"*

I don't think it worked that way for the mad and brilliant Thompson. At age sixty-seven, in February 2005, after decades of *fear and loathing*, off-the-wall drugs, and being thoroughly used up, Thompson put a bullet through his head at his Colorado mountain home. I can't imagine the smoke from that fatal shot was the *cloud of smoke* he had in mind. And I may be wrong, but as he squeezed that trigger I don't think he shouted, *Wow! What a ride*!

Poet Edna St. Vincent Millay left us an intimate testimony:

> *My candle burns at both ends;*
> *It will not last the night;*
> *But ah, my foes, and oh, my friends*
> *It gives a lovely light!*

Ms. Millay died of heart failure at age fifty-eight, leaving a legacy of rich poetry and a model of courageous, liberated defiance of oppressive male convention. To friends and admirers her life was a *lovely light*.

One of America's greatest writers, Jack London, penned these words: *I would rather be ashes than dust! I would rather my spark should burn out in a brilliant blaze than it should be stifled by dry-rot. I would rather be a superb meteor, every atom of me in magnificent glow, than a sleepy and permanent planet.*

No one ever thought of Jack London as *a sleepy and permanent planet* and his life certainly was a *brilliant blaze* not one *stifled by dry-rot*. But he died at the too early age of forty after difficult years of alcoholism and ill health.

Some of our most celebrated people lived short, painful lives, but their notes about passion still strike a responsive chord in us. I'm tempted to concede that *it all boils down to your passion*. But it doesn't. Your chances of living your best (and a reasonably long) life diminish if you incessantly burn the candle at both ends or shoot off like a rocket all the time. You live in a high-pressured, information-overloaded, helter-skelter world. Its challenges, obligations, attractions, and options are almost unlimited; your time and energy are not. So if you think it's smart to live with relentless gusto, before you know it you can burn out or collapse in exhaustion. Experience and good sense tell you that for good health, high spirit, and a reasonably long life, you need not only worthy purpose but also restful sleep, days off, changes in your routine, and, if you can, an occasional vacation.

It's clear that living up to the full intensity of life today requires you to renew your energy, and most of us are at our best when we alternate between Jack London's *superb meteor* and his *sleepy and permanent planet*. We find the desired balance when we move in and out of intense activity like high-stepping circle dancers who, arms locked, swoop together toward the center of the floor, cheering and laughing and then moving back out to catch their breath. No matter what dance you choose to do, you must withdraw periodically and become a wallflower for a while. The pause will refresh you and will let you reflect on what participation is right for your particular style of life.

An ancient Greek adage prescribes *moderation in all things*. I used to see this as an admonition not to get carried away in excess, but I now understand *all* things to include moderation. So while it may be seen as a call to curb possible excess, it also tells us to be *moderate in our moderation*. This means that sometimes it's good to keep everything centered. It also suggests, however, that life is not meant to be beige, or black and white, or flat with no ups and downs, no flair, no risks, and no failure (think of the lessons you learn when you risk and fail). Rather, it urges you to embrace life's multicolored, and multidimensional delights that abound in beauty, and adventure. Being *moderately moderate* may mean keeping mostly on even keel and tempering your commitments. But it also intends for you to unleash your passion, imagination, and daring when appropriate. You may need to take breaks, but you can't remain a wallflower forever; you must step back bravely into what Barry Woods calls the *magnificent frolic*.

If you've been stagnant for too long and your spirit has atrophied, it may help to do the unpredictable, to let the reins all the way out and, if need be, to step out of line or even out of character, just for the fun of it. Or, if you've been wildly passionate about too much, maturity may require you to pull in the reins and settle down for a time. A part of being whole and living your best life is deciding when and when not to let the reins out and to accept the consequences of whatever you do. Passion needs direction. If you aren't committed to worthy purposes such as those I noted earlier, and your fire isn't bringing out the best in you, burning out in a brilliant blaze leaves a pathetic pile of ashes.

Your goal is to make sure you don't end up with unused gifts and an *unlived* best life, so you will be smart to take *down time* for rest and repair. The Jewish Sabbath emerges from this wisdom. Wise people of all types and times have learned this lesson from both their own mistakes and from the great role models of history. Before Jesus set out on his public ministry, he spent forty days alone in the desert, wrestling with the temptation to betray his high purpose and seek worldly power. He won that match. And during his intense, three-year public sojourn, he withdrew regularly from the crowds to rest, recharge his batteries, and get his bearings.

Eighteenth century poet, naturalist, and antislavery activist Henry David Thoreau, who practiced civil disobedience against his government when he was convinced it was unjust, said, *I went to the woods because I wished to live deliberately, to front only the essential facts of life, and see if I could not learn what it had to teach, and not, when I came to die, discover that I had not lived.*

In 1930, the seemingly frail Mahatma Gandhi launched and led a two-hundred-mile march against the oppressive salt tax that was dehumanizing the poor in India. During the march, he insisted on frequent rest stops along the way where he and his companions could refresh not only their bodies but their minds and spirits as well. This dramatic act of protest shook the foundations of the British Empire and, while the name Gandhi became associated worldwide with courageous activism, he was known equally as well at home for his practice of meditation.

The passionate and courageous Martin Luther King Jr., in his crusade against racial injustice, disobeyed civil law to make things right and was imprisoned for his actions. He used his time behind bars as a respite from the rush and press of life and for collecting his thoughts, reflecting, and writing.

His *Letter from Birmingham Jail* stands as a major contribution to the twentieth-century American commitment to social justice and personal integrity.

I suspect that you and I won't spend a lot of time in the desert, on sustained marches, deep in the woods, or in jail, trying to attain the wisdom and ignite the moral courage shown by these great men. And we probably won't affect the world for good to the extent that they did. But if we set aside reasonable times to rest, reflect and refuel, we will have no trouble finding causes, places, and particular moments to which we can bring our gifts and make our own positive contributions.

Step Six. Act as a Citizen of Planet Earth

The Internet, CNN, international military engagements, and global ecological crises shrink the world and tie all peoples together in ways not dreamed of half a century ago. As I rewrite this section in the spring of 2011, the news at dinnertime tells us that ordinary citizens of several Middle Eastern countries have carried off shocking revolutions and that several other foreign nations are suffering economic turmoil. We cannot be indifferent to these far off events, because they not only affect our national economy and our pocketbooks but also our character as a people, depending on how we respond to them.

If we are thinking at all, more than ever we realize we all are brothers and sisters in the same evolving species—or, if you will, children of God and offspring of Adam and Eve—and we all deserve respect worthy of our dignity. And we know today, that wherever people on Earth suffer oppression, it affects you and me. Anyone who wants to live fully and freely must be mindful of what Martin Luther King Jr. pointed out: *Injustice anywhere is a threat to justice everywhere.* We should also keep in mind Bishop Desmond Tutu's thought that *If you are neutral in situations of injustice, you have chosen the side of the oppressor.* So, in seeking your best possible life, it is important to see yourself not just as a resident of your state or as an American, but as a citizen of the world. And this means that to be true to ourselves, along with friends and colleagues, we must play some role, no matter how modest, in the big human dramas involving justice, peace, and the survival of our planet.

Jesus once said, *You shall love your neighbor as yourself.* His parable of the Good Samaritan makes life more difficult (he never talked about making life easy, only rewarding). The story broadens the meaning of *your neighbor* beyond one who lives next door to anyone anywhere who has been violated or suffers for any reason and *needs support and guidance you can give.* This perspective means that to be a good neighbor you abide by the principle that ultimately there are no strangers.

I've noted Jesus' impact, but you don't have to be a Christian to know that because we are all of the same ongoing, human family, we can only live our best lives if we make some effort to leave our world a place that generations to come will find worthy of celebration. It's what people are talking about when they say: *For my own sake, I had to give something back to the family, to the community, to the world that cradled me.*

Rabbi Hillel, who died about ten years after Jesus was born, said, *You have a solemn obligation to take care of yourself, because you never know when the world will need you.* And his insight is important. But get your bearings here: To love your neighbor and see yourself as a *world citizen* doesn't make you responsible *for* the world–it merely makes you responsible *to* it. So you don't need to *sweat the big stuff,* such as pollution in China, droughts in Africa, or floods in Europe. You may feel the pain of those who suffer these disasters, but you neither can prevent nor resolve them. Again, be clear: You are not called to save the world or carry the planet on your shoulders–its problems are much too big for you. And if you maintain a clear perspective on being responsible *to* and not responsible *for* the world, it can save you from what we can call *compassion fatigue.*

It's not that the world couldn't use some saving. It's obviously become *one* without becoming *whole.* That's another important distinction. Nations still oppress other nations and try to resolve disputes with guns and bombs. The archaic practice of war still dehumanizes us. The world suffers much needless death and sadness from rampant militarism, nationalism, and racism. Due to ignorance, greed, and apathy, it also now reels like a juggernaut out of control and is in danger of self-destruction. Serious observers believe we have already done irreparable damage to our environment—climate change is the major menacing sign—and all too soon it is possible the planet may become uninhabitable for our children and their offspring.

The feeble efforts you and I make as individual world citizens, I'm sorry to say, are not going to get us out of this predicament immediately. But if we add our efforts to all those working worldwide for cooperation, justice and peace, as in the spirit of the Olympics, we may create a groundswell that will push our elected representatives to a positive *tipping point*. It's also possible that God, cultural evolution, fate, or the desperate actions of nations working together may save the day–history has often taken surprising turns for the good.

What can you do for the world?

If you will think cooperatively and creatively, the answer is more than you might imagine.

At any particular time, all you may be able to do as one person is offer a thirsty neighbor a glass of water. If you want to live your best life, you must make immediate and individual contributions like that no matter how small the effort appears against the backdrop of a dying world. A father and his six-year-old son walk along an ocean beach after a big summer storm. The huge waves and churning waters have cast untold numbers of beautiful starfish onto the sand, where they lie just above the water line under the hot sun. In response to the boy's fascination and curiosity, the father explains that out of the water, the fish are doomed to die. As they walk on, the boy stops and picks up a starfish and tosses it back into the sea. He takes a few steps and does it again. And then again. This slows the father's pace, and soon, a bit exasperated, he turns to his son and says, *C'mon, that's not going to make any difference.* As the boy pitches another starfish into the water, he replies, *It will to this one.*

There are some traps here, however. Most of us acknowledge that the best principle for solving a social problem is not to put a band-aid on a symptom but to counter and eliminate the causes of the problem itself. Otherwise the problem won't go away. And trying to get at the cause of social problems is hard to do on an individual basis. You might align yourself with others, therefore, to assist the neighbor in finding an ongoing source of water, or, if the neighborhood is impoverished, join or support an organization or company that provides equipment to dig fresh water wells or, that gets governments to dig them.

Near a small town at the foot of the Italian Alps, cars often run off a high, winding road at a particularly sharp curve and fall crashing to the rocks below. Wanting to help, the town council buys an ambulance to rush the injured to the hospital and take the dead to the morgue. This goes on for a year or two, and council members feel good about what they've done. Then someone suggests that the council install effective guardrails along the high road. The council sees the light and acts. For all practical purposes, the rails stop the crashes, save lives, and render the ambulance useless.

To do things for others that make you feel good but only treats symptoms will identify you as a *do-gooder*, a title you don't want. To avoid the *do-gooder* trap and be both true to yourself and effective, you must see feeling good as a by-product of, not the goal of, your service to others. The task is to discern thoughtfully, after listening to those you want to serve, what is needed and what the most helpful response might be. Indeed, without such consultation, you may find your noble intentions do more harm than good, which can be frustrating. How to help your *neighbors* help themselves may not always be clear or easy, which can also be discouraging.

To achieve focus as a world citizen, you might adopt an afflicted country with which you already feel some connection. Perhaps you've visited one in Africa, Central or South America, or Asia, or you plan to. You can read up on that country's economic problems, health concerns, or the plight of its citizens resulting from a natural disaster or political oppression. If you can't travel abroad, perhaps you can get to know students from that country who are studying at a university near you. Again, it's good to remember that you need not act as a lone wolf. Check the Internet and Yellow Pages to find groups in your area that are working in your adopted country to end injustice, violence, or destitution.

Through the Internet, you also can find out how to volunteer for environmental groups working to preserve the rain forests, the oceans, and the ozone layer—all planetary issues. Look for the local chapters of Habitat for Humanity, the United Nations, the Red Cross, and Amnesty International (the grassroots organization I mentioned earlier with more than three million supporters and volunteers in more than one hundred and fifty countries). This Nobel Peace Prize–winner investigates and shines the international spotlight on governments that imprison and torture their citizens who express opposing political positions. It organizes international postcard- and letter-writing protest campaigns to such governments and to particular prisoners. The campaigns sometimes last years, keeping hope alive in prisoners' hearts and rattling governments until the prisoners are released or die.

You also might plug into the Peace Corps and AmeriCares programs to offer hands-on assistance to people who are suffering. You can do this if you are paused between school and career or if you are retired. If you are working and approaching retirement, you might choose to retire early to volunteer or to work for small pay, either full- or part-time, in these organizations. If nothing here triggers a direction for you, get Bill Clinton's book *Giving: How Each of Us Can Change the World*.

If you are part of a community of faith, the least you can do (and it's not nothing) is ask your rabbi, imam or mullah, pastor, or priest to make sure their teachings create respect for people of all faiths, cultures, and nations that affirm worldwide peace with liberty, justice, and dignity for everyone. There may be other members who would like a channel for their concern. If so, it should be fairly easy to form a global concerns committee and create worthwhile projects.

To be an effective world citizen, it's important to be correctly informed, and I admit that it's not easy in today's world. The Internet connects us with our global community at a pace far ahead of our ability to keep up, and information overload frazzles us. This issue is compounded by the immense amount of bias, rumor, and misinformation found online. As you try to become an informed world citizen, you'll do well to keep in mind Hemingway's *crap detector*, which I mentioned in the Introduction, and cross-check your sources. It's also wise to think long term—experts are not made in two weeks—to be smart, and to bite off only what you can chew.

I realize that at the moment, you may be so burdened keeping your own life together that you cannot give one thought to neighbors, let alone another country. For now, such a limited focus may have to suffice. But it's important to know that the moment you lift your eyes beyond yourself and do something—no matter how large or small—to address injustice, violence, or hunger, or to show compassion to people who are oppressed, you will feel more deeply connected, and it will open the door to a joy you've not known. Think of the wonderful things that can happen in this world if you decide to do them, or if you set your sights on one concrete thing you can do to qualify you as a genuine world citizen.

Step Seven. Reject Powers of Death, Embrace Forces of Life

Ignorance, poverty, crime, disease, fanaticism, racism, oppression, institutional injustice, militarism, and terrorism all threaten to destroy us. A civilized society tries to counter these deadly forces, for we know from history that when they go unchecked they block everyone's ability to live their best life. But we also face other toxic powers, mostly from within ourselves and over all of which we have some control. And if we don't deal with them, they eat away at our spirit. Look at some of these powers:

> **Revenge:** History is a story of hatred, hostile attack, counterattack, and senseless bloodshed. Vengeance stalks the walkways between neighbors' homes, highways between cities, and seas between nations. Whenever threatened, our first instinct is to retaliate. When we allow a vengeful hatred to abide in our hearts, or if we unleash it violently, it degrades our

humanity, drains our vitality, and denies us our best possible lives. Under step ten, we'll look at what it takes to defeat the spirit of vengeance.

Fear: Natural disasters, disease, civil turmoil, violence, and global terrorism frighten us. We try to control them, but in the end we know we can't always succeed. You are right to protect yourself, but if you too readily capitulate to your fears and harbor them, or, by contrast, if you try to deny they're real or pretend you're above them, they cripple your spirit, contaminate your relationships, and strip you of joy. In part two, we'll look at handling the specific fears related to death and dying.

Addiction: I'm talking not only about enslavement to gambling, sex, or drugs, but also about work, play, or any pleasurable behavior we begin seemingly by free choice but at some point becomes compulsive and proves excessive and self-destructive. I'm referring to any activities we engage in to cover or avoid soul-sorrow, including that which we experience from knowing we one day will die or from difficulties in our important relationships. We know that habits designed to save us pain and sustained by an adrenaline rush can block us from doing what we most need to do, yet we readily set ourselves up for them. We often fail to nip in the bud self-destructive behaviors we see ourselves beginning to engage in, either because we don't want to face them and change, or we do but we can't stop doing them. If we become addicted, we may leave it to loved ones to badger us into getting serious treatment, or else it makes us sick and eventually kills us.

Thoughtless consumption: The advertising industry makes us feel like failures if we don't buy the latest stuff, including more of what we already have, whether we need it or not. So it's commonly chic to overspend, over borrow, and drown ourselves in gadgets and garbage and to gorge on fatty fast foods that produce obesity, diabetes, and heart disease. Sadly, those on the leading edge of instant gratification and conspicuous consumption are on the dying edge of life. We Americans have lost both the law of moderation and our ability to resist the peddlers of overindulgence.

Speed: Everything genuinely human takes a long time, except a smile, a kiss, an embrace, and a handshake. The frenetic pace generated by our competitive, complex society presses us to hurry everywhere, leaving us exhausted and empty. We have lost our ability to slow down, be idle, mull over what life means, and check how we are living. We move so fast we don't even see the damage caused by our unremitting rush, and our ability to be creative and sustain meaningful relationships atrophies and dies. *Speed kills.*

Individualism and *privatism*: We're aware that we need one another not only to help us when we face crises but also to nurture our spirits every day. Yet we isolate ourselves in cubbyholes at work, in our cars on the road, and behind the fences and doors of our homes. Our society tells us to keep our distance from people we meet, to be suspicious of them, to treat them as objects, and to exploit them as strangers. We often don't even know our coworkers and neighbors as persons.

The lowest common denominator: Much of the output from media, education, and sports is geared to entertain us, to make the greatest possible number of people feel good, and to give us what we want rather than what we need. Too often, even education and religion undermine and badly damage our capacity to live well by not encouraging us to think for ourselves. Tabloid powers glorify greed, replace wonder and excitement with gratuitous sex and violence, and encourage perverse fascination with celebrities rather than admiration of heroes.

The bottom line: Business once claimed it served people by supplying needed services, goods, and gainful employment, even as it made a reasonable profit. Today, the dollar drives almost everything. You and I are identified as consumers, greed is indeed seen as *good* by those with or seeking power and money, and corporate goals smother small businesses and determine our way of life. Rather than creative artists deciding what books, movies, TV shows, and radio programs get produced, it is CEOs in suits, thinking only of profit.

These spirit-killing powers are deeply rooted in the American psyche. If we ignore or deny them, they take control of us. In order to live your best life, it's important to see these widely accepted powers for what they are, face them head on, resist feeding them, and refuse to let them have the final say about your life. Living fully requires that you be a nonconformist. One way to strengthen your resistance and increase your personal freedom is to join with others who work to expose and defeat them. If any of these destructive powers is already overpowering you, you may be wise to get professional help.

Fortunately, you also can broaden, strengthen and enrich your life by applying the positive life forces that we have learned will nurture and assist you. If you haven't yet drawn on powers such as these, you can begin to do so.

Art: Engage beauty and interpretations of living and dying.
Community: Find a challenging, supportive spiritual family.
Exercise: Schedule walks, workouts, play, and brain games.
Fortitude: Stop any whining, face hardships, learn from them.
Friendship: Make yourself a *dispatcher and receiver of love*.
Gratitude: Show appreciation to those who grace your life.
Humor: Let your foibles and contradictions make you laugh
Justice: Honor the vision of equal opportunity, treatment for all.
Kindness: Practice thoughtful grace to everyone you meet.
Nutrition: Eat and drink properly, take vitamin supplements.
Protest: Join those who are standing up for what is right.

Simplicity: Prune excess baggage, cease impulse buying.
Self-Disclosure: Let loving family and close friends know you.
Wonder: Tap nature's *discovery channel* of awesome riches.
Work: Seek employment that benefits both you and others.

Incorporate these positive values, resources and practices in your life. Note any of them you're not engaged in and resolve to tackle one or two as soon as you can. If it isn't the last week in December, don't wait for the new year. Rather than being bored, you'll increasingly come alive. Neglect these powers, and something good in you will remain dormant, dry up and die.

Step Eight. Live in the Present.

The present is not always pretty or easy, but it's all you have for sure. No matter how cloudy it seems, as that prolific author, anonymous, writes, *life isn't about waiting for the storm to pass; it's about learning to dance in the rain.*

The past is gone. Yes, you bring from the past to the present your memories, influences, habits, and lessons, and they, along with your dreams about tomorrow, help define who you are today. The mistakes and struggles you endured in the past can act as lessons, if you will recall them and take time to reflect on them. But to live your best life, you need to not spend energy regretting the past, longing for its return, or trying to relive it.

Taking time to plan what you can of your future is another aspect of living fully in the present. The future, of course, is not real; it doesn't exist. It's a figment of your imagination, but an *important unreality.* It's that *not-yet time* that is always on the verge of breaking in and becoming the present reality. To live in the present, it is important to remember that the future of your life does not arrive tomorrow; it begins today, right now; it unfolds even as you are reading each word in the next paragraph.

Part of living fully in the present is dreaming about and planning at least the broad outlines of the rest of your life, because what you envision for your tomorrows affects your life today. So, whether you expect your future to span fifty years or only a few months, you do well to think about what you rightly need and can realistically expect from it. You would do this thinking not only so your potential doesn't slip through your fingers when the time comes but also to help you define and enrich your life today. And let me suggest that since your dying plays a significant role in your future, planning for it is of prime importance. It's also something I will try to help you deal with in part two.

Dreaming of your best possible future may call for making minor adjustments to what you currently are doing and the way you are living. It also may lead you to making major life-changes, such as relocating where you live, giving up your job or redirecting your career, or resetting the time when you will retire. It is your life to define. And it may not be necessary to remain locked into your current reality. It's not that you would need to make earthshaking changes the moment you imagined a new possibility. You will be wise to carefully review your values, weigh your options, look for sensible trade-offs and for the best times to make serious changes.

The present includes the past, which you cannot change but from which you can learn, and your past and present together can help form a future you can't fully envision or predict but can, to some degree, fashion for the better. Thus, to live in the present requires you to use the past and present to make the most of your future. It's yours to claim.

Reflect for a moment on a thought attributed to twentieth-century British novelist Arnold Bennett:

The chief beauty about time
is that you cannot waste it in advance.
The next year, the next day, the next hour
are lying ready for you,
as perfect, as unspoiled,
as if you had never wasted or misapplied
a single moment in all your life.
You can turn over a new leaf every hour
if you choose.

It's important that you understand what I do *not* mean by *living in the present*. Three counterfeit life strategies betray a lot of people. The first I call the *deferred payment plan*. It fails to see the difference between living *with* the present and living *in* the present. Under this plan you continue the unfulfilled way you presently live, and wait to begin living fully until some significant transition time you envision in your future. You waive living your best life until after you graduate, or after you get married…or divorced, or after the kids leave home, or after your health improves, or after the dog dies, or after you earn a big promotion or get that job you've always wanted, or after you retire.

You wait to live your best life, because today the world is a mess and your own situation is difficult, and tomorrow things may be easier and better. And, yes, they may be. But experience should teach us, that if tomorrow comes at all, it also may bring a more difficult world and new problems for us; and we will have settled for less than our best and wasted part of our lives. People who always put off living their best life usually end up living partially until the day they die.

A second fraudulent notion of living in the present expresses itself as the exact opposite of the deferred plan. It's the seductive approach made popular by the Now Generation, which advocates always grabbing for *immediate gratification*. The idea is to get all you can right now, for now is all you have. People who adopt this approach crave thrills today and pay little or no attention to tomorrow. To that end, they risk putting themselves in harm's way physically, socially, and economically. For example, to get what they want now, they may spend and borrow themselves into burdensome debt and jeopardize both their present and future. At the heart of the matter, they miss the point that we're not emotionally equipped to enjoy everything *right now*. Here again, from experience we should have learned that when we're willing to wait for certain things, we enrich the present with anticipation of them, and when the time comes we enjoy them more than we had imagined because of our wait.

A third inadequate strategy is living *one day at a time*. Now a *cliché*, this phrase became embedded in the American mind and vocabulary during the middle of the last century, when Alcoholics Anonymous first made it popular. It's designed to help us counter debilitating addictions. If you can't stop your self-destructive behavior through will power, this formula will focus you on getting through the present day, which is all you should try to handle. It's advocates base it on the idea that worrying about making it for a longer period of time can overwhelm and defeat you. And as Lucy tells us in *Peanuts*, *If you try to live seven days at a time, the week will be over before you know it.*

Let me note that this prescription has a rather remarkable record of freeing substance abuse addicts to maintain sobriety and hold their lives together for months and years, if not for the rest of their lives. This means, interestingly, and somewhat ironically, that to take life one day at a time is to show interest in living fully tomorrow as well as today.

Having acknowledged the value of this formula, I want to suggest that even those struggling to make it through the day would do well, at least at times, to keep one eye on the next day, if possible, because plans for tomorrow can enliven and liberate us today. As I noted, we make today better when we can look forward to a fun time, a good social or educational event, or a restful escape tomorrow, next week, six months or a year down the road. We defeat ourselves if we slavishly follow the one-day-at-a-time strategy. Under that limited perspective, before we know it, the tomorrow to which we've given no thought becomes an unplanned today that bores or overwhelms us.

Some of us find it hard to stay in the present. We sometimes get stuck on yearning for things to be as they used to be or, by contrast, on daydreaming about the future. All of us lapse into these traps from time to time, but they *are* traps, and if you are want to live your best possible life, you must avoid them. To operate fully in the present requires you to

- Dream, do what you must do to make your dream come true.

- Savor the great sights, sounds, textures, tastes, smells around you.

- Be fully present to yourself, to others, and to your environment.

- Operate at full capacity rather than doing too much or too little.

- Drop worthless and low-priority activities.

- Balance your life with work and leisure.

- Keep your long-range goals in mind.

You and I need not lament that we cannot do all of these perfectly. We can do our best and let them remind us of what we need to work on.

Step Nine. Open Yourself to Joy as Well as Happiness.

Polls suggest that Americans are wealthier, healthier, and longer living than the generations that preceded us. Though we pursue happiness as if it is our *only* inalienable right, those same polls imply we are less happy than ever.

I use *happy* to refer to the state of your spirit when you have met your needs for food, sex, employment, shelter, transportation, and money to pay your bills. You also become happy if you avoid a tragedy, outperform a competitor, or receive an award. In other words, you're happy whenever you win or get what you want.

Here are four goals that most of us think will make us happy:

1. **Wealth:** Inherit a bundle, win the lottery, marry a multimillionaire, rob a bank, or become a rock star, professional athlete, or corporate CEO who makes millions.

2. **Power:** Become wealthy, work your way up to be that CEO, an admiral, the Pope, or someone elected to high office–achieve a position of authority.

3. **Security:** Become wealthy, own a home in a safe neighborhood, invest and save wisely, marry the most

stable person who will have you, or enter a religious order.

4. **Pleasure:** Become wealthy, please your parents, light a fire under your sex life, pamper yourself, use drugs, keep entertained, and major in bliss.

Did you notice all four goals involve becoming *wealthy*? Polls tell us that three out of four students beginning college say that *becoming very well off* is crucial for their happiness. The *cliché* says that *money can't buy happiness*. One of our problems is that it *can*. It's a problem because being happy this way is often fleeting, inevitably hollow, and always at risk, realities we're aware of but ignore. We also know that wealth, which most people identify with *the* good life, does have its advantages (*I've been rich and I've been poor and believe me, rich is better*). But wealth doesn't guarantee your best life. Now is the time to give up your fixation on how much you have in the bank, what the market does, and what your estate is worth, because such a preoccupation can get in the way of creating your best possible life.

Experience tells us that, if you drop the popular but shallow assumption that to be happy you must get lots of money, you'll be free to discover a happiness no amount of money can buy. I admit I didn't always realize this. When I was a teenager, my upper middle-class parents repeatedly tried to tell me that money, or *bread alone,* wouldn't satisfy my deeper appetites. I didn't buy it. Like most kids and a lot of adults I've known, I thought that making money is what life is all about. I was impressed by the wealthy and sure that being rich myself would make me happy. Then something knocked the socks off my adolescent worldview. While doing a tenth-grade literature assignment, I found Edward Arlington Robinson's stunning poem "Richard Cory." I memorized it and it's been stuck in my brain ever since.

Whenever Richard Cory went down town,
We people on the pavement looked at him:
He was a gentleman from sole to crown,

47

clean-favored, and imperially slim.
And he was always quietly arrayed,
and he was always human when he talked;
But still he fluttered pulses when he said,
"Good morning," and he glittered when he walked.
And he was rich—yes, richer than a king—
And admirably schooled in every grace:
In fine, we thought that he was everything
to make us wish that we were in his place.
So on we worked, and waited for the light,
and went without the meat, and cursed the bread;
And Richard Cory, one calm summer night,
Went home and put a bullet through his head.

We're adults now. It is time to grow up and be clear about these matters: money does not satisfy what we call *soul*; we don't automatically become happy when we reach one or all four of the goals I noted; we are not necessarily better off whenever we get what we want; we are at our best when we want only what we need. Some people always want more than what they've got, and because they never are able to get everything they want, they are always unhappy. Others get all they want but become sated, bored and depressed: yet they stay on the treadmill of striving (Buddhists call these people *Hungry Ghosts*). Many become trapped by having their expectations rise at the same rate as their incomes, so feeling whole and satisfied with their lives remains always beyond their reach.

We also have not yet evolved into beings that find happiness by directly pursuing it. It doesn't come that way. And while the four goals promise much, they inevitably fall short and betray us.

- The rich worry about losing their wealth.

- Our elation over new *toys* inevitably fades.

- The thought of losing control terrifies the powerful.

- Security makes us feel safe but can be easily shaken.

- Sex by itself leaves us spent, hollow, and unfulfilled.

- Drugs can become addictive and damage our health.

- Fame, known famously for lasting fifteen minutes, wanes.

- Simple self-preoccupation burdens and sickens us.

In the end, most people don't know what acquisitions or achievements will make them happy, and very few realize that one way to reduce unhappiness is to reduce your wants. This last thought doesn't occur to most of us because through never-ending hype, advertisers have suckered us into believing that our primary duty is to endlessly indulge our desires.

My main point is that to live your best possible life, you need more than happiness. You need *joy*. At one level, joy is the inner richness you experience not when you have what you want or come out on top, but when you let go of the desperate need to succeed or always win, and when you're at peace with family, friends, the universe, your god, and, above all, with yourself. You possess joy (or, rather, it possesses you), when you...

- serve one or more of the eight worthy purposes I noted.

- bask in the glory of a newborn or of someone's growth.

- see magnificence for the first time in a familiar place or face.

- find awesome the Earth that gave you life and a place to be.

- celebrate the gracious gifts of time, energy and mystery.

- choose a positive spirit and refuse to let negatives define you.

- accept others as they are, and they take you in the same way.

- act in a compassionate, kind, just, or courageous way.

- make a contribution that serves the common good.

From one angle, joy appears easier to attain than happiness, for you don't have to strive for it; it's a gift you receive simply by opening yourself to it. From another angle, however, joy may be harder to come by because you cannot experience it when your base desires dominate your consciousness, when you pursue unworthy life purposes, when you manipulate others for your own ends, or when you bear that terrible burden of being preoccupied with yourself.

It may help to know that faith, hope, and love create and sustain joy. Look at this with me. When I speak of *faith*, I'm not talking about the popular notions of believing religious dogma, or *whistling in the dark*, or counting on your god to make life good for you. Here is what I mean: *Faith is confidence in your own worth that comes from knowing you are loved, which enables you to face with courage both your own hard times and the larger terrors of history.*

Note that faith gives way to courage. *Courage is not about* acting without fear—only the ignorant or foolish do that. Courage is acting despite your shaky knees, and is essential for living your best possible life. You live in a threatening, challenging, dangerous world. If you have to speak a hard truth to a boss, good friend, or spouse, mastering your fear and acting courageously may not be easy because you're at risk for disapproval and perhaps even rejection. But when you know you are loved and you matter, your knowledge will produce faith, the confidence that comes with faith will produce courage, and courage, in enabling you to act responsibly, will produce joy.

If you prefer a less complex concept with a different slant, here is one. *Faith is the stabilizing self-confidence that settles deep inside you once you become convinced that, in the end, love makes life good.* So to have faith is to claim that you already are involved in something good. I realize that life dumps on some

50

people, and faith may be hard to come by for them. Or, your life may be over-loaded or in shambles at the moment, which may leave you unhappy and not at all sure that life is so great. But when you know, in both head and heart, that you are loved and that life itself is ultimately good, faith can bring you a joy much deeper and more enduring than happiness.

Maintaining the belief that life is good is what some people mean by faith in God. Theologian Roger Shinn wrote in *Life, Death and Destiny: To believe in God means to testify that life is not a bad joke or a dirty trick... It is to say that we live in a world where words like reverence, fidelity, and love are not nonsense.* If you want joy, it's important to see the universe as good, whether you believe in the gracious ground of all being, in the evolutionary process, in fate, or in nothing more than the undeniable fact that life came to you simply, against staggering odds, as a precious gift.

Faith gives you a positive orientation to the way things are in an uncertain and often hostile world. It doesn't make life perfect, always pleasant, or fair, but it keeps assuring you that a better life and a better world are possible and worth working for.

The second spiritual value that generates joy is hope. Here again, let me tell you what I mean by a common term that we widely misuse. By hope, I'm not talking about yearning or wishing for something. That pertains to hope as a verb: *I hope you understand what I'm saying here... I hope I win the lottery... I hope my back feels better in the morning.*

The *noun* hope, however, refers to *the positive inner energy you experience when you possess a satisfying picture of the future.* Reread that to make sure you understand the difference between hope as a verb and hope as a noun. Your personal picture of the future pertains to such issues as the welfare of the environment, your country, and your city. It also concerns your close friends, marriage, family, work, and health. At any time, your level of hope varies in relation to these worlds you live in, usually with few or none of them being perfect or even spectacular. But to the degree they are satisfying or show promise, you get up in the morning to face the day feeling alive—you have hope. Even if the smaller worlds, such as family and work, are not wholly satisfying, your belief that you can make them better can give you the energy of hope and bring joy to your day.

An important point to keep in mind is that you can often do something to change your vision of the future. Some people have no hope because the prospects for their worlds are terrible and overwhelming—for example, a young, African-American man in Manhattan who doesn't have a high school education can't find a job; a Nebraska family farmer produces a crop but is unable to sell it for enough to maintain the tractor, pay the mortgage, and put food on the table; a San Francisco artist whose paintings won't sell and who, because he can't pay his rent, is put out on the street; a thirty-two-year-old mother with no husband, a brain-damaged child, and breast cancer that continues to metastasize despite radiation and chemotherapy. These folk are at a loss as to how to make their pictures brighter; they see their futures as hopeless, and they very well may be. For most of us, despite problems, we can do things to make our futures more satisfying and create hope in our hearts. And hope brings measures of both happiness and joy.

In the Bible's Chapter 13 of First Corinthians, St. Paul identifies *faith, hope and love*, as the abiding sources of joy. Impacted by Jesus, whom he claims transformed his view of what it means to be human, Paul then says, *the greatest of these is love*. I agree with Jesus and Paul—the love they talk about is supreme and it actually gives birth to faith and hope. So I've made the idea of trusting and living by this love the last and most important of the ten steps creating joy and your best life.

Step Ten. Trust and Practice Perfect Love

Whenever we try to decipher the human enterprise, love looms as our greatest prize. We intuitively know we must be loved if we are to banish our profound sense of loneliness and live our best life. Yet even as love draws us, it confounds and frustrates us, in part because its expressions seem as ephemeral as they are powerful. In Act I, Scene I, of Romeo and Juliet, Shakespeare has Romeo tell us, *Love is a smoke raised with the fume of sighs.* We confound ourselves further by using the term to cover myriad feelings, experiences, and relationships. Most of us attempt to generate intimacy based on anything that remotely smacks of love, so the loves we are counting on often can't produce it and our efforts only add to our feelings of frustration and emptiness.

Despite all this, because of love's primary position on our value scale, we must try our best to understand what the highest, or most authentic, form of love is, and what it is not. The clearer we are about it, the better we can commit to it in ways that lead to the richest of relationships and to our own wholeness.

Look with me briefly at two Greek words that have described forms of love we all treasure since early in Western history. The first, *philia* (**fill**-e-ah), identifies the natural, common affection between siblings, good neighbors, and friends. When I was in college near Chicago, I learned the Greek words that formed the name of my hometown—Philadelphia: *philia* (love) and *adelphos* (brother). I came to understand why people call it *the City of Brotherly Love.* For all of my life, this kind of love has meant a great deal to me, and I'm sure it holds importance for you, too, but such love is not deep or broad enough to complete us or make us whole.

The second Greek word is *eros* (**er**-os). *Eros* names the Greek god of sexual love (his other name is Cupid). Freud uses it to personify the life force and our sexual instincts. From *eros,* we get the terms *erotic* and *erotica,* both of which relate powerfully to sex. But *eros* is more than sex. It identifies the intense, primal desire by which we respond to everything that entices and delights us. Plato sees it as the yearning for all things beautiful and good. *Eros* taps our energy to create art and culture—that is, things, images, symbols, and sounds that are enriching in their beauty or functionally helpful.

Eros stands for our passion toward anything that attracts us or that we think will please or benefit us. When under the influence of *eros,* we don't care about the well-being of the objects of our passion. For example, we say we love mangoes, mushrooms and meatball sandwiches but in eating we literally destroy them; we simply love, or *like,* them for the pleasure they bring us.

Accordingly, when *eros* takes over sexual passion, it does so in response to those who *turn us on.* We may respect and care about these people, but under the sway of erotic passion, our primary interest in the moment is the pleasure they will give us or we will take from them. Whenever we are drawn to others exclusively for the pleasure they provide us through such things as wealth, power, or sex, we tend to see them as objects not subjects, not persons in their own right. In this way, we debase their essential human worth and sabotage the health of our relationship with them.

This is not to say that *eros* is bad *per se.* Without sensuality or erotic feeling, lush dimensions of our lives would become stale and drab, and in sexual activity the physical attractiveness of our beloved would mean nothing. It's important to affirm carnal curiosity and lust because they play a primary role in bringing and holding mates together.

It's true that in authentic sexual intimacy, lovers willingly agree to treat each other as erotic objects. This mutual granting of freedom honors sexual attraction and commitment and can turn *animalistic* sex into *making love,* the intimate act we rightly find powerful, beautiful, and worth celebrating. I should note, however, that the very willingness to make ourselves vulnerable and available as an erotic object arises not from *eros.* It comes from another form of love that we'll get to shortly. As important as *eros* is, it cannot make us whole or set us free to live our best lives any more than *philia* can. We need perfect love for that.

Before we examine perfect love, look for a moment at two powerful expressions of *eros* people mistaken for such perfection. The first is *falling in love.* We experience this heels-over-head, temporary intoxication when convinced that another person will complete our life with happiness and joy. Because it can feel so awesomely beautiful, some people *fall in love with falling in love.*

A seductive glance, touch, or kiss may suddenly knock us off our feet and cause us to fall. Or, without an awareness of an identifiable trigger, the euphoria may creep up on us over time until one day we realize we've taken the plunge. Either way, at some point we become certain that the object of our affection will give us the sense of self-worth and intimate connection that our parents first gave us (or didn't give us), that we so desperately crave, and that we don't know whether we can live without. We believe that the person for whom we fall will make us socially acceptable and special (Prince Charming will be our *star husband;* Miss America, our *trophy wife*). Whenever we *fall*, we are dead certain that if this breathtaking, absolutely amazing person will take to us, we will feel complete and live our best possible life.

Falling in love and its sustained expression—being in love—almost always includes some level of sexual attraction. We are normally drawn to someone we hope will be the lover of our dreams and dynamite in bed. This expression of *eros* is night-and-day different from *philia*, the nonsexual affection we have for siblings, children, and pals. At the same time, while falling in love feeds on heart-pounding sex, its driving power resides in the mostly unconscious reflection: *If this person will be mine, life will be perfect–I will have arrived in heaven.*

Because *eros* and sexual attraction are immune to hard reason, they often force to a back burner the logic of what is responsible and right. We need not look far to see the dark side of losing our wits and becoming unhinged in this way. People obsessed by the spell of erotic fantasy often trample on those they are known to love. No one can count the damage done to marriages and families by partners and spouses who, forever searching for *heaven on earth*, become sexually attracted to or fall in love with someone other than the one to whom they have committed themselves. It's not a calculating immorality, but, as *falling* suggests, it's an overpowering infatuation that knocks them for a loop and renders them unable or at least unwilling to do the right thing. In saner moments, we know we must handle such intoxication carefully, for we're aware that normally rational people often mismanage *eros*, make fools of themselves, and strew broken hearts across the landscape of marital and relationship dreams.

Scientists tell us that chemicals in our brain such as serotonin, pheromones and dopamine stimulate the brain's pleasure centers and create the propelling erotic force that causes us to fall in love. These chemicals generate the blissful buzz that gets us past our fear of committing to a lifelong relationship. They do so by covering our eyes (yes, this love is *blind*) to the uncongenial traits and failings of the other person that might damage the relationship (*All that matters is that we love each other!*). Sumerset Maugham says it's this kind of love that happens to people ...*who don't know each other.*

At its best, this rapturous fall enables most of us, particularly men, to make it to the altar. At the same time, we are captive to a major miscalculation in our culture regarding it. Cupid has duped us into believing the fairy tale that, because it initially draws us so passionately to our mate, it will enable us to live happily ever after. But, because *eros* by nature can be temporary and uncontrollable, it doesn't always do this; and no matter how powerful it is, we cannot rank it the number one, highest form of love.

Look briefly with me at a second important expression of *eros*. We call it romance, or romantic love. Falling in love more or less *happens* to us. Romantic love may piggyback on falling and being in love, but by contrast we, especially men, mostly have to make it happen.

Traditionally, Western women have been enamored of being romanced, and men have used romantic moments, artifacts, and tools to capture their hearts, keep them in love, and, especially, to put them in the mood for sex. We might look on romance as a way to make unbridled lust acceptable. Some male lovers are better at romance than others. Powerful hormones drive them to employ adoring notes, poetry, flowers, perfume, music, or perhaps a weekend away—which, if all is right, can offer a good romp or two, if not a couple of solid days in bed. It's common for couples to use Valentine's Day, anniversaries, and birthdays to rekindle romance, especially if the flame seems to have grown dim or died. Having once fallen in love and having believed themselves suited for each other by temperament and personality, those in a generally happy relationship or marriage find that, over decades, doing something romantic is like icing the cake. Sadly, somewhere around the 1960s, with the so-called *sexual revolution*, romance took a blow to the heart and became less and less important to sexual relationships.

For many lovers, romance still creates beautiful, important memorable experiences. But no matter how pleasurable it can be, like falling in love, romance lacks the depth to cure our inherent loneliness and to help us survive the difficult times of Intimacy and real marriage, including those of rearing children.

In the end, neither *philia* nor these two common forms of *eros* are perfect or can generate our best possible life. We must turn to another form of love for that.

Love That Frees You to Live Your Best Life

We go to a third Greek word, *agape* (a-**gah**-pay), to identify this dignifying, liberating form of love. With the biologically driven self-interest of *eros*, you appreciate others for what they can do for you. By contrast, *agape* exclusively emerges from your human or spiritual side, and compels you to respect and honor others as persons, beings of worth in and of themselves. With *agape*, you accept others as they are; they don't always have to please you, meet your standards, or fulfill some ideal image you concoct in your mind.

Agape generates genuine intimacy, the rich spiritual connection we all seek. Martin Buber says that whenever you view others as what he calls *its*— that is, not as subjects or persons but as objects that exist for your benefit, as with erotic love—you inevitably work them over to please you, killing intimacy and leaving your relationships functional at best. But if you relate by *agape*, treating others as persons—what Buber calls *thous*—you create deep, inner connections with them, making your relationships authentic and freeing you and them to be your best selves.

Some call *agape* the *law* of love, because you can expect to pay a penalty if you violate it by deceptively using others for your own ends, and because you can count on receiving internal rewards when you surrender to its impulse. We trust this law, because we find by experience that whenever we refuse or violate it, something in us sours and dies. We learn also that the more of this love we accept and give, the more we are transformed from our fractured selves into being wholly who we are.

A popular phrase for *agape* today is *unconditional love*. Take a moment to get clear on what it means. Like a coin, it has two active sides. The first is grace—the granting of favor that is unearned, unmerited, undeserved. Many people know grace as a religious term, but it also identifies everyday behaviors of which you and I, religious or not, are capable. If you give up a weekend to help neighbors move in or landscape their yard, and you refuse payment for your labor, you show them *grace*; you extend *favor* to them they didn't earn or necessarily deserve.

To be our best selves, we all need to experience grace; we need to know we are loved in spite of our blemishes and failures. When those we've offended or disappointed throw their arms around us and say they love having us in their lives, their expressions of grace generate joy in our hearts and raise our sense of self-worth. And nothing depresses us more than the thought that our future holds no promise of forgiveness and unqualified acceptance.

The flip side of unconditional love is mercy. If grace is *favor offered to those who don't deserve it,* mercy is *punishment withheld from those who do.* Originally a legal term, mercy refers to what judges exercise when they lighten or dismiss fines or jail sentences for the guilty. At a personal level, you show mercy whenever people you know violate you and you don't strike back but try to understand them and find ways to repair your relationship. Interestingly, when you withhold punishment to someone who deserves it—that is, you show mercy—you grant them favor they don't deserve, which means that all *agape,* or both sides of unconditional love boil down to grace.

As the blend of grace and mercy, *agape* not only stands as the broadest, deepest, and highest form of love, it's also the perfect love. It's perfect in that it *perfectly* meets our deepest personal needs—it accepts us the way we are and forgives us in spite of whatever we've done. It's perfect, too, because it plays no favorites; it applies to everyone equally, it leaves no one out—it won't allow us to love only those who are nice, rich, powerful, thin, talented, or sexy. In other words, it is *exclusively inclusive*. Furthermore, *agape* is perfect because we can't imagine anything better; we have no idea of how to improve it and, equally significant, we have no need to try. When we understand the meaning of grace and mercy, we can begin to see why *agape* is perfect. But this love has other qualities and expressions that can help us see more clearly its depth and breadth. Look further with me at several of these. And keep in mind that from now on, when I use the term *love*, I'm referring to *agape*.

Love reveals and fulfills your connection to all life.

When you were born, *philia* and *eros* uncovered a kinship between you, your family and everyone else, and you grew up knowing we are all tied together. If you're a typical American, however, you came out fighting not for the survival of everyone else, but for your own. Rather than emphasize your link to others, you saw an illusory separation, creating a gap between you and them. Now, when you know others accept you, care about you, and root for you, and you reflect the same love back to them, the separation fades, the gap disappears, and the connection comes clearly into focus. Your new awareness of that linkage, which was there all the time, deepens your character and brings out the best in you.

Love enables you to be known and to know.

We want to know others fully, but we tremble at the thought of being transparent to them. We're afraid that if they see through our masks to the secret self we try to hide, they will judge us negatively and even may abandon us. A friend of Marlon Brando asked him how he liked acting. Brando said he loved it, and asked him whether he could imagine going to work every day and *pretending to be someone else?* We all ought to be able to imagine that, for isn't *acting* exactly what we do? Don't we regularly pretend to be someone other than who we are? And don't we know that our pretense, which we hope will protect us, creates a gap between who we appear to be and who we really are and, thus, a gap between ourselves and even those closest to us? And don't we lose something central to being human when we play false roles?

Agape can help you drop your social facade and reveal your true thoughts and feelings at appropriate times, freeing *you* to be more authentic and to bridge these gaps. At an intimate level, with the one to whom you commit yourself sexually, it can help free you to be more of your best self. And if such love is reciprocated, it will grant both of you the power not to fear and control each other but to nurture and be close to each other.

We all know that when you disrobe emotionally, psychologically, or physically before another person, you risk the possibility of being ridiculed, rejected, or exploited. If your lover mistreats you at such a vulnerable moment, it's critical for your well being not to let her or him get away with it. But there is no other way to build a comfort zone of unity and freedom than for both of you to bare your bodies and spirits. Whenever you initiate such disrobing, it can help your lover feel closer, more open, and more willing to be vulnerable to you, deepening your intimacy. It's a rich give and take, a marvelous *agape* merry-go-round that you can jump-start simply by initiating an act of willing self-disclosure.

Love is something you do.

We think of love as emotion. That's because our affection for family and our romantic attachments express themselves in positive feelings. All love starts with emotion, but *agape* fulfills itself in respectful action, in the big and little ways you treat others as worthwhile in and of themselves, including in the bedroom. It's a demonstration of kindness, which is an amazing, magical source of joy for both the receiver and giver. No one can command you to feel a certain way, but because *agape* is the action of consideration and compassion toward others, you can be commanded to love your neighbor, yourself, and even your enemy.

By annihilating the lustful spirit of revenge, *agape* reaches the highest point of its glory in the act of forgiveness. You probably have enemies. At some time or another, they, colleagues, neighbors, or friends will violate you. Agape asks you to understand and empathize with them and not strike back. It's not enough to refrain from exacting revenge, however, *agape* requires you to forgive them. This is no trite moral tidbit for Sunday school kids; it's one of the universal spiritual laws that dictate how human life rightly works. The enlightened self-interest of *agape* requires that you be a radical forgiver for your own sake. Author Max Lucado offers insight into the act: *Forgiveness is unlocking the door to set someone free and realizing you were the prisoner.* It's an insight that we also heard from Morrie Schwartz in Mitch Albom's *Tuesdays with Morrie.* In the book, this brave man shares what he has learned about being human while dying of ALS. Because forgiveness so incredibly transforms us for the better, he tells us to *forgive everyone everything.* This law of love says, to live robustly, you cannot harbor toxic vitriol; you must forgive. You then do well to tell the forgiven friend, partner, or coworker what you've done.

In October 2006, Charles Roberts, a deranged non-Amish resident of Lancaster County, Pennsylvania, broke into an Amish one-room schoolhouse with guns and murdered ten young girls, then killed himself. The tragic news of the massacre shocked people around the world. That afternoon, the Amish began to publicly express forgiveness for the killer. Amish visitors called on Roberts' widow and children to console them. As shocking as the deadly rampage was, the Amish people's forgiveness of Roberts and the compassion they showed his family stunned the world even more. Nothing of their behavior makes any sense unless you understand *agape* and the significance of forgiveness for forgivers.

Love stands on justice.

We tend to confuse justice with revenge, carrying out punishment, or getting even (*an eye for an eye, a tooth for a tooth*). And we tend to think of it exclusively as a political, social, economic, and jurisprudence matter, because it's the basis of humane governmental policy and a liberating society. It is rooted in the view that deep down, you and I are one with every other human being, and based on human dignity and equality, we all deserve not only a level playing field in society but also respectful treatment from one another. For this reason, justice as an expression of love applies even to our most intimate relationships. It requires and allows adults who are living together to drop double standards, negotiate, and share everyday tasks based on need, skill, schedules, and interests. In marriages, it frees husbands to encourage their wives' full educational, professional, and personal pursuits. It also enables wives to support their husbands' full, equal, and different participation in the relationship. It is a tough, egalitarian love that offers you—if you are a member of a couple—hope for your best possible life, because when love shapes your relationships, it frees both parties to say: *We will live together in mutual respect and support for each other.*

Love promotes healing and good health.

Psychologists have discovered that wounded and sick people develop healthier attitudes and heal faster if shown signs of love such as calls, cards, visits, or embraces and kisses. If abused children believe an adult they deem important loves them, in spite of the damage done by their abusers, they can grow into adults who are able to receive and express love. Research in the psychology of love shows that to give caring support to the mentally ill can minimize their loneliness and fear and help them better control their sickness.

When you show respectful love to others, it helps stabilize, liberate and renew them. It also generates good health in you. When you forgive those who fail or violate you, you keep alive the prospect of a healthy relationship with them one day. You also enrich your own sense of worth and transform the quality of your own experience, all from the inside out.

Love rightly prompts you to limit your own freedom.

According to Alan Ritter, writing for the website Simple Truths, for the deepest of relationships, the 100/0 percent principle provides the formula: You take full responsibility (100 percent) for developing your relationships and expect nothing (0 percent) in return. As you operate this way, you prompt those to whom you relate to do it as well. Consequently, the 100/0 percent principle transforms your relationships to something approaching 100/100 percent. Being persistent in your respect and kindness toward others gives you the best chance to change the dynamics and depth of your relationships. With your persistence, breakthroughs occur for the persons involved, their families, and their organizations.

The intimate relationships you cultivate may involve discomfort that comes from the other person's *baggage*, whether material, emotional or psychological. *Agape* understands this and requires you to be patient with intimates and leave their freedom intact. To love this way may mean hardship and sleepless nights and may limit your own freedom to do what you want to do. Why would you do this? Because when you give up control and pseudo freedom for authentic intimacy, you gain the more *genuine* freedom to do what you need to do to be fully yourself. Most people just give up too soon. Want to live your best possible life? Practice the 100/0 percent principle.

Love multiplies itself.

Every time you are graced by others, your love for them increases. If you dare to pile grace upon grace in return, you make such love flow more deeply between yourself and them, adding to your joy and theirs. And your love—not guilt or obligation–moves them to reciprocate, which, once again, prompts you to return their love and pass it to others. In this way, we can all produce endless chain reactions and cycles of mutual benefit, because being loved is the root structure and life-energy source for living fully. Think about this: You live your best life not by becoming rich, powerful, or famous, but by being loved and being able to love—it is love that frees the authentic you to emerge. And strangely (here's the real marvel), the more love you give away, the more you possess, or are possessed by that love, *even if others don't return it.*

Love stays alive even when unfulfilled.

Whenever you express philia, eros, or agape to others, you hope your love will boomerang back to you within agreed upon boundaries. When it does, it enriches you. But when you express philia or eros toward another and no love comes in return, you are left cut off and unfulfilled. With agape, however, you can live with joy even when love is not returned--that is, before fulfillment arrives. It keeps you caring for those who are dysfunctional and even harmful to you and themselves; it lifts you through the not yet of relationships, even when your heart is broken.

Accordingly, *agape* keeps you caring for those close to you who are dysfunctional–it lifts you through the *once was* and the *not yet* of relationships, when connection has been lost, turned sour, or remained undeveloped. What this love asks of you in such relationships requires no mean trick. It calls you to stay with others through their repeated failures *without* attempting to control them, *without* letting them become dependent on you, if at all possible, and *without* letting them destroy either themselves or you. And you love in this way with no assurances, only glimmers of hope, that one day you'll enjoy their sense of self-worth restored and your relationship fulfilled. In the meantime, through ongoing disappointment, your patience rewards you with the satisfaction of treating them with respect.

Make certain you are clear about this–*agape* doesn't ask you to let others abuse you. Don't interpret Jesus' command to *turn the other cheek* to mean you should do nothing when mistreated. In this small but extraordinary metaphor, Jesus rejects revenge, retaliation and violence in response to maltreatment and offers in their stead, nonviolent resistance. In his public ministry he exhibited the genius of this effective tactic; and in more recent times we've seen its power in Gandhi, Martin Luther King Jr., and many others.

While normally thought of as a political tactic, nonviolent resistance applies also to relationships. When others violate you and, rather than either striking back or doing nothing, you *turn the other cheek,* you call attention to their abusive behavior and put both moral and social pressure on them to stop. If you resist them without striking back, if you let them know you will not tolerate their abuse and, especially, if you also tell them you forgive them, it can shock them into facing their abuse for what it is, and to stopping it. In that most shocking, yet rational act of *forgiving everyone everything* that Morrie talks about, you hasten the healing process and increase the possibility of renewed relationships.

People who abuse often know they've done wrong but want to continue to do it anyway. So if you turn your cheek when others violate you, they may not try to change, or they may try but immediately fail, or they may stop for a while and then fall back into it. If any of these occur, you can tell them that, even as you forgive them, you deem their behavior unacceptable, you will not tolerate it, and you are breaking the connection with them that enables them to do it. Then you make that break. You do this, because you know it does neither them nor you any good to let them continue. And it's another way to show them you love them.

Love lives alongside and inside of *philia* and *eros*.

I grew up in a middle-class household comprised of my parents, three older sisters, my father's mother, my mother's brother, and me. I'm sure, as with every family, we were dysfunctional to some degree, but none of us was abused or afraid for our safety or went to bed hungry or cold. My family loved me, and I loved them in my own immature way.

When I was twelve, my good fortune made a quantum leap. A summer camp counselor sat down with me one morning in Pennsylvania's Pocono Mountains and explained the significance of grace and mercy. I was running my preadolescence on the acceptance and affection of *philia*, and as a preteen entering puberty, I was beginning to feel the power of *eros*—my sexuality was kicking in and all my juices were flowing. That morning, a bright light went on in my head and heart about the compelling notion of *agape*. *Wow!* The insight forever changed how I look at and feel about others and myself. I don't mean that *agape* replaces *philia* and *eros* in my life—they remain important to me. And I'm certainly not implying from that day on I fully express this love. I'm saying that in seeing *agape* as the source of human connection, I now actually *want* to love in this way and consciously will myself to do so. Over the years, I've become clearer on *agape* and am better able to measure the degree to which I express it in a wide range of human encounters.

With everyone you meet, *agape* starts with expressed welcome and acceptance (*I take you the way you are*), moves to different levels of verbal affirmation (*I appreciate your gifts and your efforts to express yourself*), struggles with differences and shortcomings (*I'll work at understanding your weaknesses as well as your strengths*) offers support (*Lean on me—we can get through this together*), and, at its deepest levels, frees you to forgive and to care without reservation (*I'm never going to forsake or abandon you*).

Love becomes most authentic not in the easiest of relationships, fortified by *philia* and *eros*, but in the everyday grind of interaction with people who tick us off—those who snub us, think they're better than we are, make false charges against us, act irresponsibly, disappoint us, try to manipulate us, or express opinions we think are stupid, silly, wrong, or harmful. The point is we pass the *agape* test when we can treat such people with respect, understanding, and compassion, even when they don't recognize it or reciprocate. And every time we pass this test, it testifies to the splendor of human capability.

I am contending that *agape* is the first, central, and last word to be said about your humanity; in depth it sits at the *ground and heart of your being.* It also stands above you as the ultimate definer of what it means for you to be truly human. This is, of course, why the modern Hebrew-Christian tradition reaffirms the notion that *God is love.* I'd like to put it this way, however, in a question: *Might this perfect, transcendent, creative love be God?*

Death may face us with the ultimate mystery of our existence but a*gape* is our central mystery. We can't explain where it came from or why it was already here when we arrived, why it is so absolutely crucial to our welfare, or why no one can define it with any finality. At the same time, it is not some secret in the far reaches of the universe that only those with higher mental powers can access. It's the power available to free all of us from the fear of being imperfect, to lift us to face our struggles with courage, and to make life work for us. When all is said and done, this mysterious, mind-boggling love is the critical key to living our best possible life.

Other benefits flow from placing your ultimate destiny in the hands of this mystery of love. Not the least of them is that whenever you think about your eventual death–especially if you have good reason to believe it is imminent–your joy will not be diminished by fear of cruel punishment by a vindictive God. There is no room in a world defined by *agape* for a sadistic deity.

If you are approaching the end with a terminal illness but are conscious and able to interact with persons around you, *agape* can enrich your last days. It can do so not only if they express it to you but also, paradoxically, if you demonstrate it to them. You wouldn't express love to impress them with how selfless you can be at such a difficult time, but to make sure you share your last hours with companions of joy instead of despair—it's an authentic and legitimate demonstration of enlightened self-interest.

Unfortunately, whether facing life or death, most of us focus more on *philia* and *eros* than on *agape.* We spend more time on shallow, functional relationships, doing unimportant tasks, being passively entertained, and buying things we don't really need than on cultivating our capacities for giving. In part, it's because our culture encourages self-indulgence. In its better moments, it may honor sacrifice and philanthropy, but it relentlessly pushes products and sensual pleasures. And all of this sells us short. To stop conforming and being your own worst enemy, you must buck the social tide and make sure you put love first. You may take the nine other important steps we've discussed, but if you fail to place your life in the hands of love and practice it, achieving your best life will prove impossible.

Here is a checklist for taking the ten steps. Before you go any further, mark a star to the left of the numbers of the steps you've already taken. Put a question mark to the left of those you haven't taken but are willing to work on. Later, as you take those steps, you can put a star next to them, too.

1. Integrate Three Basic Models for the Human Journey

2. Adopt a Positive View of Life That is Realistic

3. Claim an Important Level of Freedom for Yourself

4. Choose Life Purposes that Ennoble and Empower You

5. Engage Life with Both Passion and Good Sense

6. Act as a Citizen of Planet Earth

7. Reject Powers of Death, Embrace Forces of Life

8. Live in the Present

9. Open Yourself to Joy as Well as Happiness

10. Trust and Practice Perfect Love

In challenging you to take these steps, I've been asking you to let go of any narrow perspectives to which you may be clinging, to open your mind to the broadest of viewpoints, and to make wise choices in redirecting your life. Now I'm asking you—no matter how strange you may think the idea—to explore with me in part two the fascinating notion that knowing you will die one day can help free you to live fully right now. In the pages ahead, I'll be elaborating on six creative approaches to intensify and enrich your life in the face of your inevitable death. So, while on the surface we will be dealing with dying, we still will be consumed with how you can live your best possible life.

Final Farewell

This is your final mortal day.
No more creepy tomorrows and tomorrows.
You're ready to slough off your mortal coil.
Now you can make the best of it;
You'll get your medication this evening
And then that long sleep from which no one returns.
Fear, of course some fear is normal.
For those of strong faith
It's a mere transformation.
For those of little or no faith,
Or Pascal's wager,
You can choose your own reincarnation.
Morbid? Of course not – it's part of a natural process.
Now it's a matter of style.
How do you wish to depart?
A whimper or a bang is for poets –
How about a knowing smile?
After all, living and dying is a continuum
Of the same procedure; full of stresses and pleasures,
Highs and lows, but mostly in between.
Now for way of exit;
Do you prefer satin or linen sheets and soft pillows,
Or silk pajamas and your initialed robe?
Bed or your favorite rocking chair and flannels?
No jeans! Dying is not casual.
How about just a sigh?
Good Bye.

Ben Slomoff   October 2010

I want to die in my sleep like my grandfather… not screaming like all the passengers in his car.

Will Shriner

The primary source of soul-sorrow is the fear of death.

Edward John Carnell

Imagine there's no Heaven
It's easy if you try
No hell below us
Above us only sky

John Lennon

We obsess in this country about how to eat and dress and drink, about finding a job and a mate. About having sex and children. About how to live. But we don't talk about how to die. We act as if facing death weren't one of life's greatest, most absorbing thrills and challenges. Believe me, it is.

Dudley Clendinen, dying from ALS

PART TWO:

KILL THE GRIM REAPER

Three Ways to Face Dying That Don't Work

One thing you know about yourself is that you are designed to live—you embody the powerful, universal life-instinct. And you are human—the most fascinating expression of life we're aware of and one that is forever trying to defend, sustain, and advance itself.

You also are dying, headed for death. Every moment something is born in you, something else is passing away. You are fighting a losing battle against dying—it is the final certainty of your existence. You and I are *on the clock* because the breath we're inhaling right now, like those we've drawn in the past, is part of an ongoing countdown to the last one we'll ever take. We owe it to ourselves to live this day as if we are in the process of dying, because we are.

So far I have been using the terms death and dying almost interchangeably. They do not refer to one and the same reality, however, and it will help us to understand the difference between them. Death is the state of non-being, or at least of not being alive as we've been. Dying is not a state, but is the dynamic process that transports us from life as we know it to the state of death we really have not experienced and don't know. We focus on both realities in this second part of the book, for the inadequate ways most of us respond to each of them stops us from living our best possible life.

Fortunately, most of us don't dwell every day on our dying. We know that we can no more keep a steady eye on death than we can on the sun. Sadly, the mentally ill, the chronically depressed, and the debilitated elderly often focus incessantly on little else. Their morbidity forms the uncreative, unconscious,

71

desperate way they deal with the fact that they one day no longer will be. Some become haunted and so paralyzed by their obsession with dying they cannot enjoy living. The grim reaper has defeated them, robbed them of their best life.

I don't want you to live this way. I also don't want you to spend your days at the other end of the spectrum, denying and ignoring the fact of your eventual dying. Most people live at this end who are healthy, economically stable, and anticipating satisfying days to come. With their fairly good fortune in life somewhat established, any grim reaper looms as *the great spoiler*. Thoughts of dying generate a dread in them that can darken their brightest hours. Unhampered by cruel burdens, they seek the everyday distractions of sex, sports, business, religion, entertainment, virtual worlds, and other pleasures to stave off the terrifying thought of dying, refusing to consider for a moment they could draw their last breath before the sun goes down or the clock strikes midnight. For most affluent Americans, denial is our style; it's our inadequate strategy for dealing with dying, our ultimately feeble weapon against the grim reaper, a pathetic fraud we perpetrate against ourselves.

A particularly popular and acceptable diversion or form of denial deserves its own category. Many people deal with dying and death by escapist fantasy. They try to avoid the devastating power of death by clinging to the vision of a wonderful afterlife, such as the Hindu reincarnation of the soul, the ancient Egyptian spiritual rebirth upon death, the Native American happy hunting grounds, and the Christian's blissful heaven with Jesus above the sky. It's their way of trying to kill *the grim reaper*. We'll look closely at the issue of an afterlife later.

For now, I hold that denial, morbidity, and afterlife fantasies are inadequate ways of dealing with dying and death. They stop us from coming to grips with them, and from living authentic lives. They simply don't work. I propose a multidimensional one that does.

A Fourth Way That Works: Six Important Approaches

The strategy I propose for dealing with dying and death offers creative approaches to help you deal ably with their scary side and free you to live robustly with integrity in the real world. Even if you've never heard of these six approaches, or you have and have carefully put them off, I urge you to open yourself to them so no matter how much time you have left, you can live your best possible life and die your best possible death. Begin at the ending.

Approach One: Accept Your Dying As Inevitable

When our four children are young, my wife Barbara and I spend three summer weeks every year at the same spot on beautiful Lake Almanor in Northern California's Mt. Lassen region. Its a great break from work and school. The adults spend mornings playing tennis or golf while the kids join friends at the recreation area. In the afternoons while they swim, Barbara and I relax on the beach, reading or chatting with other vacationers. We often barbecue in the evenings in the grove by the lake with tennis friends. I especially enjoy schmoozing with George Stewart, the tall, lanky summer tennis pro at the lake, a business professor at City College of San Francisco, and a sometimes lovable curmudgeon. We are both parents of teenagers.

Over the years, George says many things to provoke my thinking. None strikes deeper in my brain than his response one afternoon to the answer I give when he walk up to me on the beach and asks what I am working on. I tell him quietly, *I'm preparing for a class on death and dying I'm going to lead in the fall.* He takes a step back, pauses for effect, looks me straight in the eye, and as if lecturing and wanting everyone on the beach to get his point, shouts, *Godammit! Every sixteen-year-old ought to know that one day he's going to die!*

I think birds suddenly stop singing, parents' heads turn and eyes open wide, and children cease their laughter—few of us are used to hearing such profane proclamations shouted out in peaceful social settings. I'm immediately wondering whether anyone else agrees with George. I do, for I think it's clear to anyone who is looking, that teenagers are able to process death as a final reality and are old enough to understand they are not immune to dying. Unfortunately, most adults don't talk to them about it. And most sixteen-year-olds play out their days as if they're never going to die. So do most thirty-six-year-olds. A lot of sixty-six-year-olds do, too.

Why is it so critical to stare mortality in the face? The answer comes in a simple paradox: *It will make your living better.* When you realize you'll never see this day again and you may never know which day will be your last, you'll cherish each as a priceless gift and will be eager to live it fully, whatever that may mean to you at any given time. If you believe your dying is forever far off, then today means little and it won't matter that you live it poorly, for there is always tomorrow. Film actor Michael Landon, whose doctors tell him at a too early age that he is dying, warned, *Somebody should tell us right at the start of our lives we are dying. Then we might live life to the limit, every minute of every day. Do it! I say. Whatever you want to do…do it now. There are only so many tomorrows.*

Living every day fully requires us to take seriously the issues we talked about in part one, but it also demands that we squarely face the fact we're mortal.

In the summer of 2011, the United States' population topped 312 million. On October 31, 2011, according to the United Nations, world population passed seven billion, and was growing steadily at about seven million a month. Every hundred years or so, a turnover of human life takes place on the planet. You and I have been given the privilege of participating in that cycle. Nature will run its course and we will be—we *must* be dead on schedule, or at least after what we call *a natural lifetime.* We might wish this were not the case, but think what it would be like if we all were to stop dying. The world would soon suffer a catastrophic population explosion, the social order would collapse, and people would be on a rampage to kill one another over an increasingly limited supply of land, food, and water. In other words, our current problems would be exaggerated to the extreme; and the living would envy the dead.

As far as we know, no one's made it past one hundred and twenty-two years, one hundred and sixty-four days. As of July 10, 2011, there were six living *supercentenarians* (age one hundred and ten or older) who had reached their one hundred and fourteenth birthday—three in the United States, two in Japan, and one in Italy. The oldest living person on that date was an American woman named Bessie Cooper, aged one hundred and fourteen years, three hundred and eighteen days. It has been calculated that one person in two billion will live to be one hundred and sixteen years old (to use an apt metaphor—*don't hold your breath!*).

The 2010 census reported that there were seventy-two thousand Americans aged one hundred or older, almost double the 1990 figure of thirty-seven thousand, and sixty-four American women and eleven men were *super centenarians*. I'm told that one in five thousand Americans now reaches the one-hundred-year mark, and that 85 percent of them are female. Again, the odds against you are extremely high, especially if you're male. If you make ninety, male or female, the odds are that your life will soon be over. Our lifetime warranty has an expiration date, and, for the vast majority of us, it's before our ninetieth birthday.

What are we to make of this? You may sympathize with Robert Ettinger, who wonders if being born isn't a crime, *why must it carry a sentence of death?* When put that way, maybe there are no satisfying answers or explanations, unless the biblical notion that we die because our first parents sinned against God makes sense to you. Whether it does or not, every thinking adult is aware of the fact that all of us must one day serve such a sentence—no one gets out of this world alive. So whoever it was that said, *I intend to live forever... so far so good*, really wasn't saying anything of significance.

If we are honest with ourselves, we know we are going to die, because a variety of reliable sources tell us that everyone from centuries before us is dead and gone. We also know of people around us who are aging and dying everyday and, intuitively, we know that the mortality rate remains 100 percent. By logical deduction, we come to this undeniable, intimately personal, rational conclusion: *All humans are mortal. I am a human and therefore I am mortal.* Then we put a lot of time and energy into denying this *undeniable* conclusion.

At its deepest level, denial is rooted in an unconscious assumption that having our lives snuffed out ought not to have a valid place in the scheme of things; it simply is not right—we are born to live with the instinctual desire to go on living. We hold that living is right but dying is somehow not only undesirable but also wrong.

As a society, we deepen our denial by making death a social taboo, a subject not discussed in polite society. Actually, we consider death a sign of weakness and bad taste. The terminally ill often feel embarrassed and obligated to apologize for their dying, as if they are rude and ultimately failing their loved ones. On top of this, other than some arts and sciences, the major powers in our culture—including politics, entertainment, business, education, medicine, and religion—shield us from the reality of dying and fail to challenge our refusal to accept it as inevitable. As a result, though we do know that death is definite and universal, few of us deal directly and creatively with it, even when it draws close.

Someday scientists may employ genetic manipulation, caloric restriction, and embryonic stem cell reprogramming to stave off the ravages of aging and disease and extend life expectancy by as much as several decades, perhaps longer. Until then, like everyone else, you and I are terminally ill and our body has its own time limits, beyond which we are not going to go. The fact is that you and I are going to die in this century, and, as I write this line, nothing we or anyone else can do will help us escape it.

An old story about a merchant's assistant in the Baghdad Bazaar (yes, *that* Baghdad!) goes something like this: While waiting on a customer late one morning, the young clerk suddenly sees the dark figure of Death, the one we call the grim reaper, moving toward him. Almost at the same moment, Death catches sight of the clerk. He suddenly stops, takes a step back, and stands staring at him. Stricken with fear, the clerk dashes through the back door, jumps on his horse, and gallops through the city and out its north gate into the hot desert. He rides hard all afternoon to the city of Samarra, where, at dusk, totally exhausted, he takes food and lodging at an inn. As he awakens the next morning, he is terrified to find Death standing silently at the foot of his bed. On his knees, he apologizes to Death for running from him, claiming he had been shocked to see him the day before in Baghdad and had panicked.

Death says, *Ah, yes, and I was stunned to see you there, for I was well aware of our appointment this sunrise hour, here in this faraway city of Samarra.*

We'll come back to the grim reaper and discuss the problems presented by belief in him. For now, we'll simply let this story represent a reality important for us to grasp—that we cannot escape our eventual dying.

You'd think that in the twenty-first century, we 'd get over denial of our mortality—but we haven't. Its persistence may be due in part to the fact that life expectancy in America has nearly doubled in the last hundred years as a result of so-called miracle drugs. Also, some religious folk unconsciously engage in denial because they can't get out of their minds the ancient notion that we'll be held accountable for all we've done or not done in this life, and they're anxious, if not terrified, as to whether they'll pass the test.

Whatever the cause, we do what we can to put off thinking of that inevitable ending until we've at least lived what we call *a long life* and are so weary we're ready to let it go. Even then, most of us resist facing the reality until it stares us in the face. Ironically, educated people think of themselves as members of an advanced, rational, sophisticated society, yet go to remarkable lengths to avoid being reminded of dying and death. We...

- celebrate and emulate youth while disparaging old age

- dress cadavers in finery, use cosmetics so they look asleep

- label any talk of death as macabre, offensive, and unnecessary

- employ euphemisms: *She passed away; he went to his maker*

- discourage and squelch public displays of grief and mourning

- stop fatally ill patients from referring to their dying

- use dehumanizing means to keep alive those who are dying

- let loved ones die isolated in institutions rather than at home

- live today as if we'll always have another tomorrow

Part of our problem is that we rarely see dying up close. Most of the 80 million people worldwide who will die in the next year will do so in relative obscurity. It's estimated nearly 80 percent of the 2.5 million or so Americans who died in 2011 drew their last breath heavily medicated and out of sight, in hospitals or nursing homes. Most of us never have watched someone die or touched a dead body. I suggest we are missing something of great value.

I remember the first time I was called to a home where a man in his fifties was dying. His wife, associated with the church where I was the pastor, phoned when his breathing slowed and became unusually labored, and I went to be with them. Her love for him was palpable. The two of us sat holding his hands for an hour or so. Finally, with a few short, heavy gasps, he drew his last long breath. The room instantly became quiet. I could see new tears in the wife's eyes and felt them in mine. I was aware of the sudden absence of the beloved life that had been there seconds before, and I was struck by how unusual and somehow sacred that moment was. I was intimately connected to love as it faced the final mystery. From then on, each time I was called into a similar situation, I reminded myself of the privilege I'd been given. Death had lost its intimacy and significance for most people I knew, and I didn't want that to happen to me.

It's true that in movies and on TV we see images of people dying all the time, but they seldom portray dying realistically. In the typical story, the good guys survive and the bad guys are almost always killed by gunfire or other unnatural means. Seldom does a film's story dwell on the pain of people who are dying, allowing us to empathize with them or, equally important, to feel the anguish their loved ones must endure. Rather than evoke our natural sympathy, most movies present killing and death with such dispassionate harshness that we see it as unreal and not worth taking seriously. Most of us don't lose a moment's sleep after watching actors die on television.

We also keep death at a distance by not speaking about it around home, especially when children are present. In the public sphere, where outside voices come into our homes, politicians, entertainers, and other talking heads on television avoid speaking about death whenever possible, though it often cannot be avoided when a public figure dies. Comedians sometimes break the taboo. Look at some of the witticisms widely attributed to Woody Allen:

> *I've no problem with my death; I just don't want to be around when it happens ... The difference between sex and death is that with death you can do it alone and no one is going to make fun of you ... The thing I'm going to regret most about my memorial service is that I am going to miss it by a few days ... I don't want to achieve immortality through my work—I want to achieve it by not dying.*

I know that humor can be used as a form of denial about death, but at least Woody is actually talking about the subject, which is one step toward bringing it closer to home. Here's the point: Failure to talk about our dying and death reinforces our denial, and denial stops us from dealing with what's real—and that dulls our lives and puts a clamp on our growth and freedom.

When doctors tell patients they have only a limited time to live, as was the case with actor Michael Landon, it almost always increases their passion for life. Yes, the news shatters some, depressing and incapacitating them. But it invigorates many more, who then try to live their last months and weeks as fully as they're able. They may use their time left to take care of unfinished business (more on this later), and to fill and empty their own *bucket list*. It's what psychiatrist Irvin Yalom was talking about when he said that while the very fact of death destroys life; *the thought of death gives us life.*

This paradox infers that if we openly acknowledge the *ever-present elephant in the room*—our own mortality—we will live more fully. We will

79

want to develop character, honor the deepest mysteries of life, live with as much panache as possible, maintain relationships of integrity, seek life-giving knowledge, take care of our health with rest and recreation, contribute to justice and peace in the world, and demonstrate love to all we meet.

The longer we shield ourselves from the central truth of our existence, however, the more we distort the lens in our mind's eye and become captive to a consciousness so clouded we are unable to sort the important from the trivial. We buy stuff we don't need, engage in mindless activities, and chase after social status and other inanities. Denial ranks at the very top of human folly because it stops us from living our best possible life.

When someone close to us dies, reality jumps back into focus. Even the knowledge of people dying whom we don't know can help penetrate our denial and straighten out our vision and values. On September 11, 2001, international terrorists killed more than three thousand innocent civilians, mostly Americans, at Ground Zero, at the Pentagon in Washington and in the woods of western Pennsylvania. Most of us didn't know any of the victims personally, yet much of what you and I thought was important earlier that Tuesday morning blew away like dead leaves on a windy fall day.

Television images of those passenger jets penetrating the World Trade Center towers, and of people just like us leaping from the top floors, embedded themselves in our minds. As we first witnessed those images, an awareness of our own mortality sobered us. The importance of our intimate loved ones and concern for their safety quickly rose to the fore and changed our priorities radically, if only for a while. Today, many of us are a bit less in denial and a bit more human because the events of 9/11 forced us to stare our own mortality in the face.

Early in this millennium, other tragic events have made our inevitable death a fact rather than an abstract idea: Hurricane Katrina; the AIDS and SARS epidemics; wandering refugee mothers with their starving children in Darfur; the Iraq and Afghanistan wars; Middle Eastern suicide bombers; the devastating quakes in Southeast Asia, Pakistan, India, Haiti, and Chile; and the catastrophic earthquake, tsunami and nuclear radiation release in Japan. If we have been listening and looking, these happenings have brought awareness of death and dying to our consciousness.

The testimonies of those who go through near-death experiences can make us look at life differently and alter our priorities. In 1999, internationally renowned art critic Robert Hughes, then sixty-two, totally demolished his car in a horrific head-on collision on a desert highway in Western Australia. When police tried to extricate him from the wreck, Hughes begged them to shoot him if his car caught fire. After five weeks in a coma and a dozen operations, he spent nineteen more months in the hospital. Not given to sentimentality or piety, Hughes says he emerged from his trauma with an enhanced sense of *how wonderful life is and how precious each day is*. He claims his recovery taught him how powerful the human will is; it became for him a positive personal truth. He also says he gained the sad insight that we almost have to die to realize how much we have to live for, because we don't seem to gain it simply from living.

Hughes is right. If you agree and affirm his insight, you need not wait for *the harsh light of disaster* to realign your priorities and live fully. You can make peace with your inevitable death and use it as an ally, a *teacher of wisdom* that enriches you. How do you create and sustain this kind of consciousness? It depends on your level of knowledge about death, how well you can resist slipping into denial, and how much it means to you to live your best possible life. You might take at least one step from the following list, and, if it doesn't prove valuable, take another and then another until you are getting the help you need:

- Search the Internet or your local library for books and articles that deal honestly with dying and death.

- Read newspaper obituaries and ponder what values the deceased lived for and what you hope people will say of you after you die.

- Watch DVDs of *Saving Private Ryan*, *Wit*, *Tuesdays with Morrie* and the HBO series *Six Feet Under*. They offer vivid, honest portrayals of people living heroically in the face of dying.

- Go to the memorial service of someone who was important to you and reflect on how the positive and negative aspects of that person's life and death might affect the way you live.

- Write down what you'd do and what you'd say to loved ones if you knew you had only one hour left to live.

- Try to imagine your death—its most probable causes, when it might happen, what it'll be like. Then list things you might do as it nears and what you can do right now to prepare yourself for it.

- Contact your local hospice program to volunteer to be with terminally ill persons in a supportive role. People who do this find the work hard at times but deeply rewarding.

- Each morning, look in the mirror and say to yourself: *This day is another gift. In a few hours, it will be gone forever. One day, you will have no more hours to live. What will you do to treat this day with utmost respect and live it wisely?*

I don't suggest you take all of these steps before the week is over, but taking any one of them will remind you that you are not the only one who will die, and will help you gain some measure of coming to terms with your eventual death. It also will help you to be fully present to both others and yourself.

Most of us would like to reach old age. We think one good thing about being old is that you know you will never die young. We're not too sure we want to *be* old, however. My friend Dorothy, who is in her seventies, says, *The good news is that with nutrition, exercise, and modern medicine, we're living longer. The bad news is that with nutrition, exercise, and modern medicine, we're living longer.*

We're living longer in better health these days. We're also living longer with the knowledge that we are dying. When we make it *over the hill* and life winds down, many of us feel as though we are trudging uphill in sand, carrying heavier and heavier weights. Every day something reminds us that we're aging and that our end grows nearer: the aches of arthritis; knee, shoulder, or hip problems; cataracts; some form of cancer; physical skills that inevitably diminish; and yes, eventually, everyone's plight–the diminishing of sexual function. Because even in our later years we're generally afraid to entertain thoughts of dying, when the time comes many of us are unprepared to face it directly and creatively.

Fortunately, a life force also is at work in us. Despite denial that tries to make dying seem forever distant, voices regularly speak to us from the back of our brains, the pits of our stomachs, or the bathroom mirror, reminding us that all too soon, in a few years or decades at the most, we no longer will be. This declaration is nothing new; humans always have heard it. Still it annoys us, because it assaults our basic instinct to continue living and our fears associated with dying and death (we'll look these fears in a bit).

Here's the task: Appreciate this voice. It's trying to warn you; it's pressing you to fully live the days you have left. You also can congratulate yourself, because this good voice is your own. It's your authentic, inner self, reminding you not to let its promptings get lost in the clamor of daily pursuits.

I trust you can see that I'm doing you a favor by prodding you to listen to this valuable voice and to look at your eventual death more honestly. Be clear: I'm not recommending that you take every breath as if it might be your last, because you can't live your best life at any age if you're morbidly obsessed with dying. I'm also not suggesting you stop living because one day you're going to die anyway. Rather, I'm urging you to start living by cultivating an ongoing awareness of the inevitable, final life experience—your dying. I want you to know what it means to live each day so it's good enough to be your last.

I urge you toward this awareness, for if you forget you are headed toward what Gore Vidal calls *the door marked exit*, you betray yourself. Nothing will help you to live your best life more than seeing that one day you'll no longer have the chance.

My good friend Bobby, who is eighty-eight, lost two of his dearest men friends in the past few years. Just about every chance he gets, he recites Robert H. Smith's poem, *The Clock of Life*:

> *The clock of life is wound but once*
> *And no man has the power*
> *To tell just when the hands will stop*
> *At late or early hour.*
> *To lose one's wealth is sad indeed.*
> *To lose one's health is more.*
> *To lose one's soul is such a loss*
> *That no man can restore.*
> *Today, only is our own.*
> *So live, love and toil with a will.*
> *Place no faith in tomorrow,*
> *For the clock may soon be still.*

Approach Two: View Dying as Part of a Natural Process

When people today live into their seventies or later, and they die after a period of disease or decline we moderns tend to acknowledge their deaths as natural, as part of the order of things. If anyone is surprised by such a death, we say, *She died of natural causes… His body had been breaking down and he was due to run out of gas… She had a family history of cancer.* We are tempted to ask: *What did you expect?* Not many of us today accept the notion of demons, or satanic forces invading the human realm to kill people, as our forebears centuries ago believed. We know that it's nature that limits everyone's days.

Dr. Sherwin Nuland, in his award-winning book *How We Die*, reports that our vital organs and bodily mechanisms shut down in various ways, depending on our age, or the disease or the mishap we suffer and when they do, we die. None of the collapses, he tells us, is pretty. When our heart stops pumping blood to our brain or it can no longer receive blood, the awesome organ dies its own death, and we die with it. None of us, Nuland points out, will outlive our brain, and our last living act will be to die, no matter what kills us and at whatever age.

As a pastor, I frequently was called to be with elderly people when they were seriously ill or dying. I came to understand that positive attitude, or spirit, were important to sustaining life, but that no matter our optimism or good spirit, when the body's key organs fail to function, we soon die. I remember vividly years ago being with a hospitalized man in his eighties. For some time he has valiantly fought a debilitating lung condition but given no specific directions regarding the medical care he wants when beyond a cure. Now, under medication, he lurches in and out of consciousness, suffering pain that makes him tear frantically at the straps that are taped to his arms and that tie him to his breathing machine. The man's wife and son are beside themselves watching his agony. His doctor is torn. He wants to keep the man alive but his attempts to relieve his suffering have failed. He believes that if his patient could survive without the machine, which he doubts, he would have no life to speak of. He confers with the wife and son. They painfully concur that to be most humane, they should take him off the machine.

The doctor and a nurse disconnect the tubes, while the three of us stand by quietly, holding hands. The man struggles briefly, then gasps once or twice before his head falls heavily back against the pillow, and then he is still. Our eyes are now glued to the digital monitor above his bed, which counts the beating rate of his heart. With the disconnect, the numbers on the screen immediately plunge from seventy-two to forty-five, quickly bounce back up to sixty, then down to the forties again, and over maybe fifteen seconds, to thirty-five, eighteen, twenty-seven, ten, four, two, and finally zero. The diminishing numbers bear stark visual testimony to his heart shutting down without oxygen, a natural source of its life. The flashing zero on the screen brings tears to our eyes and relief to our hearts. While the doctor and the patient's family make a decision that affects the timing of the man's death, none of us sees his dying caused by anything other than his age and his disease.

It's unlikely that you and I will perish as victims of war, crime, or international terrorism—reports tell us that only about one in twenty-five Americans today dies from human violence. Likewise, the odds are against our dying early from an earthquake, a Category 5 hurricane, an airplane crash, a car collision, an overdose of a drug, or an *underdose* of food. Actually, if you are over fifty, and especially if you are not reckless and live responsibly, the odds are highly in favor of your succumbing in old age to a chronic illness such as heart disease, cancer, diabetes, or Alzheimer's.

Of course, real forces outside ourselves, including societal violence, disease, toxic chemicals, and the ever present power of gravity, can take our lives when we don't want them to, including long before we have had a chance to live a full life. Despite awareness of these common powers, whenever someone dies unexpectedly, we tend to explain the untimely death as the work of a mysterious purpose-driven, supernatural being. Even when an older person dies from an accident, or suddenly from a fatal disease, we resort to that strange understanding of death as a plotting enemy, an intrusive, hostile adversary to be dreaded and avoided at all costs.

In the fifteenth century, the English began personifying death as the grim reaper. He continues to emerge in the darker side of our western mythology as a skeletal figure carrying a large scythe and clothed in a black cloak with a hood. We see him not simply as existing to escort the deceased to some *other side*, but as the one who actually causes the death. As portrayed in the Baghdad tale, like a stalker he relentlessly tracks each of us down, and then he cuts us down with that scary scythe.

Let me note several reasons why we should do away with, or *kill*, the grim reaper. First, making death into a superhuman-like figure encourages people to think they can bribe, trick, outwit, or bargain with him and, thereby, escape their own dying. Serious effort to get the reaper to pass you by can take your attention away from the critical need to maintain your health and to design and live your best possible life.

Second, belief in the grim reaper can lead to an irresponsible fatalism. To believe your dying is inevitable is important, as I've already stressed. But it's not the same as believing you can do nothing about its timing, nature and cause. We have all heard stories of people who escaped dying in an accident or from a potentially fatal disease, and they say such things as, *It must not have been my time,* or *I won't go until my time comes.* But people die every day from smoking, overeating, excessive drinking, reckless driving, failing to exercise, and not taking care of their health. A supernatural, outside force has nothing to do with the deadly results of these behaviors, which we can avoid, for the most part, if not by willpower alone, with help from supportive friends and health professionals.

Here's another reason to discredit and eliminate the grim reaper. It has been found that in people who are sick and close to dying but are medically treatable, belief in the grim reaper may lead to frightening hallucinations of him that actually cause their death prematurely by destroying their confidence they can survive the crisis.

Perhaps the most fundamental reason for killing the notion of a grim reaper is that he doesn't exist.

Many religious people reject the idea of a grim reaper who determines when and how we die. They attribute the work to God, particularly as dying pertains to believers, the righteous, the *saved.* They say things like, *He took her to a better place,* or, *In his own good time God called him home.* In other words, they believe that *the good man upstairs,* not the scarey, mythical figure dressed in black, does the dirty work of death.

But the problem remains: The pious may portray the one who causes our dying as a benevolent God rather than a malevolent enemy, but the work is still done by a foreign, supernatural power, and this leads to a lot of denial, distraction, failure to deal with reality, and panicky bargaining (*Oh, God, if you get me through this, I promise I will...*). And though such escapist fantasy may make some believers feel better about their dying, there is no evidence that it helps them live their best possible life.

The earlier story of the Baghdad clerk hammers home the point that we can't escape our dying. That's all well and good; it's an important truth to take to heart. Unfortunately, it also perpetuates the nonsense of a grim reaper. The truth is that regardless of what causes your death at whatever age, all evidence points to the fact you will not die by the hand of either a benevolent or grim *reaper*; you will die because nature has doomed your heart, lungs, and brain— the key physical organs that sustain your life—to malfunction, break down or wear down and fail when diseased, damaged or exhausted with age. Doesn't the fact that everyone and everything dies assure us that dying is included in the natural rhythm of life? Although they go through an entirely different kind of death, even the stars die.

I am pressing the point it is important to see dying as part of the natural life process. I break the process into four stages:

Stage one begins the moment we are born. In this earliest life stage, we already are fatally ill and moving toward death. This isn't fantasy. Our planet's ecology includes biological processes that extinguish human life. Our cells, as in every living organism, are programmed to age and die. They simply run out of steam, unable to divide anymore. Every day, tens of thousands of brain cells peter out, diminishing our capacities and shortening our life. Even so, in this first stage, while from time to time we may suffer from illness, injury, or abuse, most of us remain physically and mentally functional most of the time. Thus, physicians who attend to us, our closest friends and family, and we ourselves think of ourselves as living rather than dying, which strikes me as a good way of looking at it. At the same time, every day we live, we die a bit.

Stage two begins when illness, injury, aging, or medication downgrade our health and quality of life to the point we no longer can maintain vigorous relationships, feel functional and useful, or enjoy the ways we spend our time. Our doctors say we are more *dying* than *living*. Most Americans enter this stage toward the end of the normal life span. They do so by crossing the often imperceptible line that separates it from stage one. Depending on how far we move into stage two, we still may be better described as *living* (stage one) rather than *dying* (stage two). Movement back to stage one may depend on our genes, a nutritious diet, the effectiveness of our medical treatment, the state of our immune system, the resilience of the natural healing process, and our willful spirit—*the puzzling potential of inner strength*. We may go back to the first stage and even back and forth several times between the two. Such a stage can last days or months or longer. Toward the end of an extended time in stage two, we may find ourselves unsure of whether we want to live or die. Again, most of us won't face this stage until our later years.

Stage three ushers us, usually quickly, to death's door. We may cross this critical threshold from stage one or stage two as a result of the long-term effects of cancer, a sudden heart attack or serious stroke, an unexpected injury, an overdose of drugs, smoke inhalation, or drowning. At the very end of this stage we may be drugged and semi-conscious, in a coma, or in a persistent vegetative state supported by extraordinary medical procedures, unless we've restricted their use ahead of time. It's possible that stomach pumping, CPR, the Heimlich maneuver, drug injections, or breathing machines may move us, at least temporarily, back into stage two, and even stage one. Moreover, the body has been known to repair itself mysteriously or undergo a sudden, baffling, but marvelous reversal of condition, what religious people are eager to call a miracle.

Stage four arrives if medical efforts fail and the *miracle* doesn't happen. At this point, the heart is unable, for some reason to pump blood, the lungs no longer support breathing, and *brain death* begins. This process takes seconds or at the most a few minutes. At its completion, a doctor, paramedic, or family member, despite knowing that the cells in the body are still alive, no longer says we are dying but reports we have *expired*. Simply put, we are now dead and gone.

In summary, the four stages of dying are

Stage one: deteriorating physically, invisibly, every day

Stage two: enfeebled by advanced age, injury or disease

Stage three: at death's door, medically beyond help

Stage four: heart, lungs, and brain shut down, life ends

Studs Terkel, a longtime Chicago radio personality and author, published his thirteenth book, *Will the Circle Be Unbroken?*, shortly before his ninetieth birthday in May 2002. It contains people's poignant testimonies about their experience of dying, and he said he learned a lot from them. At that same time, Terkel diligently worked on his fourteenth book, *Hope Dies Last*. He said people would often ask him, *Do you have a deadline to finish it? Deadline?* he says he would shout in amazement: *I'm the damned deadline!* Terkel knew what he was talking about. He saw his dying as the end of the natural life process, and both his age and body told him he didn't have much time left. In his case, it was six years.

Here is the critical step: Kill the grim reaper in your mind by making the mental shift to view dying as natural a process as being born. It's an intelligent step to truth, wherein you say to yourself: *I no longer will look on the grim reaper as real but will face the fact I am a mortal being programmed in my cells to die when my brain dies.* Growing up requires this shift. No more Santa Claus, no more tooth fairy, no more Easter bunny, and no more grim reaper.

Approach Three: Face Your Fears

All animals have a survival instinct, so it's normal not to want to die, and to fight or flee if someone or something threatens to kill you, especially if you have not yet lived a long life. To kill the grim reaper is not to escape dying and death, which is impossible; it's to stop your fear of them from dulling down your life with soul-sorrow, and from terrorizing, capturing, and immobilizing you when something forces you to think about them or when your dying stares you in the face.

You can diminish your fear of dying by accepting the fact that it is natural rather than the result of either an impulsive or a strategic act by some supernatural power. To see that the natural order does not play favorites, that it claims absolutely everyone and not just you, can also counteract this fear. And you can further steal some of its power by standing up to it, as it were, staring it in the face and grabbing it by the throat, rather than ignoring it, pretending it's not real for you, or trying to run from it.

Look at several fears that feed the fear of death and dying and what you can do to diminish their power.

The fear of the unknown: Much about dying and death is a mystery we never will understand fully, but even partial knowledge can be critical, for even the hardest of truths can help free us from fear. Unfortunately, when we know something is wrong with our health, most of us tend not to want to know whether it's as bad as we suspect. It is good to know that patients whose doctors explain their terminal illness to them, tend to find the threatening diagnosis better than being left in the dark. If you must face a serious illness, even small steps to increase you knowledge of it can be helpful. Medical information from respected sources such as the Mayo Clinic lies at your fingertips through the Internet, and your doctor should be a phone call away. You can cross-check the information you get from each with the other. Knowledge gives you a measure of control, and control helps diminish fear.

The fear of being abandoned and humiliated: The terminally ill often end up getting cut off from the world. We cringe at the thought of dying alone under glaring fluorescent lights, *bare-assed* in a starchy paper gown, with a body or mind ravaged by disease, surrounded by well-meaning but functionary strangers. Dying inside the bleak medical machine is a prospect sharply in contrast to that of spending your last days in a favorite room at home, buoyed by the warm physical contact of loved ones and the gentle ministries of caring hospice workers.

Those who die while lovingly supported feel connected to the *agape* at the center of life. They feel esteemed and secure and are therefore more at peace with their death. If it bothers you to think of dying in a sterile hospital setting, explain now to family your desire to have personal support at home when the time comes, if possible. If you have no family, sit down and talk with your closest friends and draw up the proper papers that will enable them to care for you. If you have no close friends, you can begin reaching out with genuine *agape*, making the acquiring of them your number one priority.

The fear of untreatable pain and suffering: The prospect of dying a slow, agonizing death haunts most of us. Throughout the several thousand years of recorded history, dying meant to the vast majority of humans suffering long, drawn out illnesses and excruciating pain in the third and fourth stages of dying. Life, as it still is in parts of the world, was brutal, and maintaining good health was difficult. I confess that when I think of dying accompanied by unnecessary suffering or being slowly tortured to death the prospects terrify me. You and I can't know for sure, but chances are very good that we won't have to suffer such brutality and humiliation. At the same time, we know that one day an accident or disease may impose on us the suffering of protracted, excruciating pain. Fortunately, medicine can alleviate 97 percent of the pain you might face and allow you comfort, if not a thrilling quality of life. I suggest it is good to ask—or even press, if necessary—your doctors as to what specific palliative care will be available to you in the eventuality of such a plight. And if present channels and resources for such care are limited and inadequate, perhaps you can do something now to change that. Then fill in an advance medical directive, stating for loved ones and doctors what you'd like done if you face such a predicament.

The fear of dying before you have lived a long, full life: You can't ahead of time claim for your life the biblical life span of *three score and ten,* or even of one more day, no matter your age. But if you are young in America today, your probability of living well into your later years is high.

Four things favor your living a long life (even if you are in your eighties, there may be something in this section for you). First, due to better prenatal care, biomedical achievements, safer cars, and more education about nutrition, Americans enjoy the longest life expectancy in history: almost eighty years. In the twentieth century, it increased by three decades, and experts predict further increases over the next hundred years.

Healthy habits are second in terms of living a long life. They include eating nutritionally, taking daily multiple vitamin supplements, drinking alcohol only moderately or not at all, not smoking, getting adequate sleep, exercising regularly, and going in for annual physical exams. Despite someone's opinion that health nuts are going to feel stupid someday, lying in bed dying of nothing, these sensible practices give you a good shot at enhancing both the length and the quality of your life.

Third, chances of living a long life are increased by your freedom to be sensible about the risks you take—a jackass has to act like a jackass, but you don't. Risk is a part of living robustly, but you don't have to be reckless. If you've been foolishly putting yourself in harm's way, you can stop.

The fourth condition for longevity–and by no means the least important–is living a worthwhile life. I gave meaning to the term *worthwhile* under step four in part one, where I identified eight purposes worthy of your life. If you've not yet chosen one or more of them, you can go back to them now. If your sole concern is how long you will live, fear of death will maintain too much control over you. How you live is just as important as how long.

The most elegant strategy is to live creatively and productively for however much time you have. No one in his or her right mind wants to die too young, but no matter how long you live, it's critical to make sure that before you enter the third and fourth stages of dying, you've not shortchanged yourself by living a shallow, directionless, mediocre, or do-nothing life. What you've read so far has been geared to help you avoid just that.

Most of us in this fast-paced culture bank on repetitive acts to avoid laboring through a long decision-making process every time we turn around or want to take a step. Our automatic mechanism clicks into gear, we get into a groove, and we save ourselves time and energy. This automation also can trap us, however. We can so mechanically grind through our days that we become locked-in and never stop to ask whether what we are doing is the best use of our limited time, whether that's five months, five years, or half a century.

The linear view of living I talked about in part one suggests that we live fully only if we reach old age. Thus, the idea of dying early terrifies young people. But length of life, while important, is not everything. Many who make it into their nineties don't feel fulfilled, don't find their later years pleasurable, and don't die happy. Studies show that people faced with dying before old age often handle it well if they've been loved and don't think they've wasted their lives.

With some irony, if our health and lives are generally good, when we face the third stage of dying, no matter our age, we will grieve the thought of missing out on what we've been enjoying—the embrace of our children, the companionship of a spouse or lover, kind friends, days free of pain, and the feeling that we matter to the world, or at least to those whose lives we touch. The richer our lives are in these ways, the greater our grief may be when our death draws near. Young or old, such grief pales in comparison to the pain of never having felt whole or never having lived your best possible life.

The fear of leaving unfinished business: You can quell this fear by giving appropriate time and energy to important personal matters and keeping them up-to-date. Unfortunately, this idea won't help if you put off getting your life in order *until you think you have more time to do it.* To avoid this mistake, write down right now those things you'd regret not having done if you were to learn today that you are going to die tomorrow. Then start working on the most important of those items now. We'll look further at this idea under the next approach to dying.

The fear of eternal damnation: If no one ever threatened you with the doctrine of hell, you may want to skip the next few paragraphs. The idea of a god punishing his children forever has many ancient and medieval sources steeped in superstition and fear. Today, in the West, evangelical Christianity and its popular fundamentalist offshoots keep the idea alive. You may have come under the spell of a religion that told you that if you don't keep God's Ten Commandments, if you don't go to church or synagogue every week, if you don't pray a lot, if you don't trust Jesus to save you from your sins, or if you think about sex too often, you can count on God banishing you to the unquenchable fires of hell, where you will be tortured forever by the wicked fallen angel Lucifer and his demons. (I don't know about you, but the prospect of eternal fire strikes me as infinitely more dreadful than simply *not being* anymore.)

If you've suffered through this kind of teaching, you may suspect you have failed to impress God or even ticked him off. If so, you may not be consoled to hear that you will be joined in *the lake of fire* by billions of God's other children who have broken the Ten Commandments or who haven't trusted in Jesus (including those who have never heard of the commandments or Jesus). Misery may love company, but there's a limit to the solace it offers, and the doctrine of hell has wreaked horrific havoc in many a life.

I was taught this primitive idea of hell as a preteen, but I never really got into it or feared going there. Originally, that's because, of course, I was told I went to *the right church*. Later, as a youth, I became smitten with Jesus' good news about *agape* and began questioning how I could reconcile it with hell. Into my adult years, studying the issue and doing my own thinking, I eventually could no longer bear the childish notion of a loving God who tortures forever his disobedient children, and I deliberately chose not to believe in the devil, demons and hell, because the notions struck me as superstition and total nonsense. I let it all go just as I let go of Santa Claus, the tooth fairy, and the grim reaper. And I feel joyfully liberated for having done so.

I simply have turned over any question of life after death to *agape,* the transcendent love we discussed in part one and the reality that grounds me. Dying appears regularly on my radar screen, for I live in a large retirement community. I don't like the idea of my dying as long as I'm well and able to enjoy life and contribute to the world (you'll hear more about this in approach six and in the two postscripts) but fear of eternal damnation doesn't touch me.

This is not the result of a scientific study, but my experience tells me there are three types of persons who are *not* troubled by the thought of going to hell: (1) those never taught the doctrine or had it used on them to control their behavior, (2) those raised on the threat of hell but who, when they became adults, put their thinking caps on and couldn't put love and hell together, and (3) those who believe in hell but think they are so righteous that no god would ever send them there.

If religion introduced you to hell, it's possible you have dismissed it as archaic and stupid, which a lot of religious people have done. If so, you may now be happy believing in *agape* as the absolute reality that is worthy of your complete trust and loyalty, or reason as a key to human fulfillment, or in some combination of spiritual insights and practices that give you a sense of wholeness, or in nothing at all. Or perhaps you are unhappy, but you are still looking, having found nothing that ultimately satisfies your mind and heart.

If you were reared on hell and have intellectually written it off, unfortunately, it may still lurk within you emotionally, especially if you feel guilty because you aren't perfect or don't live up to your own realistic expectations of yourself. So it is important to see that, though you no longer hold it as a conscious belief, buried in your psyche it can erode your vitality and rob you of joy and your best possible life. Such negative effect can diminish with time, especially if you rebuild your worldview on enlightened insights that ring true to you about human nature and a universal, unconditional love. But if this negative power is dissipating too slowly, or you are aware it interferes with your joy, when you finish reading this book, you will do well to get professional help in working it out. We'll look further at hell and what follows dying in approach six.

The fear of being a coward in the face of death: It's understandable that this fear might trouble you, because you've heard of people who died badly, even shamefully. Then again, you probably haven't faced or practiced facing your death, and you may have botched challenges far less daunting than making a graceful exit from life. But this is one of those fears that fades when we acknowledge it. If you are afraid of not dying bravely, admitting it to yourself, and to loved ones, gets it out in the open and helps dissipate its power.

It may help to know that you are probably braver than you imagine. Most of us are not as bad at meeting life's moral and spiritual challenges as we think we are. September 11, 2001, showed that ordinary citizens—people like you and me—can act with extraordinary courage. No doubt, this fear of acting cowardly, along with their vocational commitment to save strangers at the risk of losing their own lives, compelled those police and firemen on 9/11 to enter the World Trade Center's burning towers. At least it suggests they might have preferred to be dead heroes rather than living cowards.

For many of them, strengths they didn't know they had came to the fore; they rose to the occasion and were bravely heroic in spectacular ways. Moreover, history tells us that people who live worthwhile lives and who stare their basic fears in the face usually do not die as cowards. And if you deal with the fears I've already described, you will disarm much of this fear and, when your time comes, you will be better able to cope with your death.

Over the years, whenever I got over a miserable cold or case of the flu, I would say to friends, *At first, I was afraid I was going to die, then I was afraid I wasn't.* That remark, springing from how awful I had felt physically, was the way I reminded myself—with a feeble attempt at humor—that though we look at dying as the greatest threat to our humanity, we can identify experiences that may be worse. Here are a few of them:

- **Extended, excruciating pain.** When faced with unavoidable suffering, people often look for a way to die as quickly and as painlessly as possible. Some of those trapped on the upper floors of the World Trade Center on 9/11, rather than die agonizingly by burning, chose to leap through windows to a certain but more immediate death. The fatally ill, rather than endure ongoing, unbearable pain, often opt for strong painkillers, knowing the drugs may hasten their dying. And because we see terrible suffering as worse than death, people lobby for our right to euthanasia and doctor-assisted suicide.

- **Being humiliated, abused, and rejected.** Many minority persons know how painful this is. Homosexuals and transgender people know it, having been made to feel shame by self-righteous heterosexuals for what they are and guilt for what they do. Many find such social abuse so horrific they take their lives rather than bear it any longer.

- **Having no hope of ever living a decent life.** Young people chained to drugs or poverty, or in prison for life, often possess no potentially satisfying picture of the future—the basis for hope I described in part one. They become so beaten down or have so squandered their lives that they deem dying more attractive than going on with life. Only the powerful life instinct makes some of them choose to live another day rather than die.

- **Feeling as if you don't matter to anyone**. People who have little or no *agape* in their lives, who are lonely with others all around them, or who suffer from low self-esteem, mental illness, sustained depression, or addictions from which others have broken free, often feel not only unworthy of life, but also worthless; and for some of them dying is preferable to living.

The young and middle-aged understand the fears I've been talking about, but some older people are unafraid of death and are ready, and even eager to die. They anticipate death as a relief from anxiety, depression, excruciating pain, poverty, or some other terrible burden. They have put their affairs in order and are ready to go, without fear of death and at peace with themselves and their dying. They are fortunate in that they don't have to hold on to life too tightly and are free to let nature take its course, particularly if they think they can be saved from needless suffering. Even younger, well-off people may reflect at least fleetingly on death as a way to escape medical, marital, moral, business, or financial problems.

Most of us, at least at times, have mixed feelings as we stand before the great mystery. Hamlet says, *To be, or not to be, that is the question.* I hear him struggling with whether it's better to go on, bearing his heavy burdens, or to take his own life and step into the great unknown. In the freedom of our secular democracy, we will continue to struggle with whether Americans have the right to end their own lives or to assist loved ones who, with good reason and sound mind, want to do so and need help. And, if one day we decide they do, there will be no end to discussions of how society can best monitor and support the exercising of these rights.

Those who attend death and dying seminars often want to know what it will be like to die, how they will feel and act if they know it's near, and how their loved ones will respond. Once trust is established in the group, they inevitably let go of the inhibitions and talk about being afraid. As the seminars end, they commonly testify to the fact that when they can talk about their fears, they experience deeper levels of liberation from them. To live free from these kinds of fears, we all need friends to whom we can talk about them, persons who will listen without negatively judging us. I'm suggesting we take the first step toward such liberation when we are honest with ourselves and others about what we fear.

Are you getting the idea that while you may not be able to freely choose when or how you are going to die, you can make choices that will affect how you experience your death? In one sense, we're just getting started.

Approach Four: Vow to Die with Minimum Regret

Even educated Americans seldom think of this simple, profound notion: When it comes time to die, make sure all you have to do is die.

The wisdom here applies to everyone. While some of us will live long enough to realize that our death is drawing near and will have time to take care of business, many of us won't. An old axiom says you ought to so live that *no matter when you die, you won't have to look back with regret.* Of course, because none of us is perfect and all of us have made mistakes we can't undo, we have things we regret; and we do well to accept our imperfections and learn from our mistakes. In one sense, having no regrets about your life might mean either your memory has politely faded or you've been too cautious or tame in your life. Vincent van Gogh said that if you never had anything to regret, your life would be *very empty.*

But we're not talking about mistakes you made in the past. We're focused here on not going to your grave kicking yourself for not having done well by your own best interests and those of your loved ones. We all owe it to ourselves to take care of business today that is important to them and to us so that when we find ourselves dying tomorrow we don't burden them and end up ourselves with unnecessary regrets.

According to those who work with dying people, many express regrets that they didn't have the courage to stay true to themselves, that they lived in ways they thought others expected of them, and that they kept their good and bad feelings bottled up. A regret that concerns almost all of us pertains to our failure to stay appropriately in touch with family and friends and to resolve rifts between our loved ones and ourselves. Sadly, some people are so busy trying to stave off their dying that they not only are bereft of wonder and passion, but they also leave unhealed wounds in their most intimate relationships. Christopher Morley once said that if we all had only five minutes left in this life, we would jam the world's phone lines, *stammering to others that we love them.* That's sad. The idea is to be true to yourself by expressing that love now rather than putting it off. When you can do that, you will know something about living your best possible life.

You'll avoid another common regret by settling specific, practical matters. These might include a written health care directive that covers what you want done if you contract a fatal illness and are hospitalized. If your heart stops, do you want to be resuscitated? If you slip into a coma or vegetative state, do you want heroic measures taken to keep you alive? Dr. George Burnell, in his book

Freedom to Choose: How to Make End-of-Life Decisions on Your Own Terms, offers specific guidance on how to have your wishes carried out and how to save your family conflict, expense, and legal entanglements after you die.

Practical matters also involve the passing on of your material possessions and the settling of your estate. Your estate may not be significant now, but one day it might be, and you don't want to be an undue financial burden to your loved ones after you die. If you own property or have investments or assets, I urge you to see a lawyer now about a living trust. If you can't afford a lawyer, go online and fill out a form of will that will be helpful to those you leave behind.

You can designate what you want done with your remains when you die: They might be donated as transplants or for medical school purposes (made possible by the Uniform Anatomical Gift Act), cremated (in California, check the Nautilus and Neptune societies; elsewhere, Google *national cremation*), or buried. If you would like to be buried, consider an eco-friendly *green* burial in which you leave behind nothing more than biodegradable compost to feed plant life (look up *natural burial* or *green burial* on the Internet).

You can plan your memorial service or gathering—where it should take place, the persons you would prefer lead it, what music and readings you may want, and so on. You will help loved ones if you write this down and give the information to the executor of your will. Keep a copy in your safety deposit box and make sure you tell those closest to you where the key is.

My oldest sister, May, after several heart problems, died at age eighty-eight in March 2008 after a long and active life in the Philadelphia area. She left behind two sons and two daughters, two sisters younger than her, and me—her little brother. All of us are fairly well set in our lives. She donated her body to the medical school at the University of Pennsylvania (a positive contribution and no funeral costs). And while she was not a woman of great means, she instructed her children to use the first few thousand dollars of her estate to hold a memorial party for her many relatives and closest friends. In May of that year, forty-five of us gathered from far and near for our own *May Day* to celebrate what she meant to us. We brought hundreds of pictures to a fine luncheon, where we shared our memories and feelings, shed some tears, had a few laughs, and toasted her in appreciation of her life. I'm convinced she died satisfied that she'd graciously taken care of business and had no serious regrets.

If these concerns strike you as too remote because you're young, think again. No one is immune to dying early or suddenly. Even if you feel no urgency to tie up the loose ends of your life, I encourage you to take a small step or two in that direction. It may help to see how important it is to settle these matters by looking at them from the position of *receiver* rather than *giver*. If your parents are still living, they may have unfinished business. If that's the case, you might talk respectfully with them about it. For example, if you've received no instructions from them about extreme medical procedures, you can initiate a conversation: *Mom, Dad, if you've never signed one, I'd like you to fill out an advance health care directive so I'll know what you want in the way of medical care if you ever become critically ill. If your heart stops, do you want it restarted? Do you want doctors to keep you alive no matter what? We assume, rightly or wrongly, that if your heart stops, you want medics to try to restart it. Is that right? And what about putting you on a breathing machine?*

If they welcome your concern, you can help them find a directive form (search for advance health care directive on the Internet), through which they can stipulate their health care wishes. You might also help them with setting up a living trust and writing a will. Going through this process with them should give you experience to apply to your own life.

Again, it is critical to recognize that you cannot separate life and death and that life is really preparation for the third and fourth stages of dying. I've already suggested that you prepare best by living fully, which includes taking care of business as it arises or as soon as is reasonably possible. Unfortunately, too many people don't think of settling their affairs until the second and third stages of dying, when their doctors tell them they have only a short time to live. Sadly, for many of them it is too late. You can sit around lamenting what you've failed to do or you can strive to put these matters out of your mind. Neither response liberates you. If you take care of these issues now, you'll be more at peace when you face the end. If you wait to take care of them until you're sure your time is near, you owe it to yourself to have *very good timing*.

Actually, no matter your age, you can decide now what your priorities will be for the rest of your life, even though things will change and you may have to make adjustments. Here is one way to do it. Start with the eighty-year life expectancy figure (or something close to it) and calculate the time you think you may have left, barring an unforeseen misfortune. If you are under fifty, break the time into ten-year blocks and give each one a blank page, writing year numbers at the top (2020 to 2030, for example). If you are between fifty and seventy, use five-year blocks (2020 to 2025). If you are over seventy, you may want to use one page to represent one or two years (2020 to 2021).

Select key words for your major life involvements, such as *family, friends, work, community service, recreation,* and *travel,* and write them down the side of each page. Leave space between them, and under each note, enter goals you think you can reasonably reach in that particular time period that will help you avoid regret. Consider these goals your priorities. You can always go back and change them, but make it a commitment that until you do change them, you will not give much time to anything that doesn't contribute to accomplishing the goals you've listed. Every few months, check your progress and make any changes you think are needed. Such tracking can give you a sense of accomplishment, conquer depression, and go a long way to helping you both live well and die at peace.

Surveys report that most old people at the end of their lives say they most regret not having reflected more, risked more, and made more positive contributions that would live on after they die. People facing death often confess disappointment at not having fully embraced the wonder and beauty of their lives, the universe, and the world. Hafiz, a Persian poet of the fourteenth century, vowed to avoid such a lament:

> *One regret dear world,*
> *that I am determined not to have*
> *when I am lying on my deathbed*
> *is that I did not kiss you enough.*

Society does not offer many good role models for dying, and, if you're typical, you haven't taken much, or any time to practice facing your death, even though you know you may enter the fourth stage of dying with no warning. You can't prepare perfectly for your death, and you no doubt will end up with some regrets. You can minimize these, however, by the choices you make right now. If you work at it, you will feel much better about yourself–not simply when your dying draws near, but now–by knowing you're doing your best. It also may help to keep a sense of humor about being imperfect, like the person who said, *I have come to terms fully with my own death. I also can walk on water and fly like a bird.*

Approach Five: Prepare to Die With Dignity

We all are aware that the third and fourth stages of dying *can* be horrible and humiliating and we know that some ways of dying are worse than others. You do not want to be killed by an immoral, insane, irresponsible, or criminal act such as drunk driving, medical malpractice, a drive-by shooting, or terrorism. You also don't want to die prematurely in a helpless state, such as in drowning at sea, being trapped in a burning building, or being stuck on an airplane in a long, downward plunge to earth. (I've always felt that these are among the worst ways to have your life end.) At any age, the thought of dying in these undignified ways is a nightmare. Fortunately, your chance of perishing from any one of them is very small, and, because we now live longer, most of us more than likely will die of old age or a fatal illness in our later years. That doesn't mean it will be easy, however.

Along with living our best life, we all want to die what people call *a good death*—a dignified dying with merciful delivery from the horrors of prolonged suffering or the indignities of dementia and dependence. Those who study death and dying tell us that, at one level, people usually die the way they live. If you live well—that is, if you find your passion and *calling* or work that fulfills you, if you are authentic in your relationships, and if you make appropriate contributions to others—you have a good chance of dying at peace with yourself and with life.

We should not talk about dying well as if it is something easily arranged or always possible. According to Dr. Nuland, most of us will not get to choose how or when we die, and a *good death* with *dignity* is a relative rarity. He insists that there is little that is dignified about the breakdown of our bodily systems and vital organs as we enter the third and fourth stages of dying. Whether they collapse from the ravages of cancer, a heart attack, a stroke, or some kind of accident or assault, he says they present neither a pretty picture nor an enjoyable experience. According to Nuland, this means we must not talk glibly about *death with dignity*. What we *can* do, however, is focus on aspects of dying other than the physical ones. We may have to face the *dark night of the body*, but we can give light to what commonly is called the soul, or spirit, or consciousness.

Part of the reason a dignified death is rare is that most people don't think about what it means, let alone make preparations for it. Right now, here, we can do both. We can reflect on what a good death is and give ourselves the best chance to attain it. Marjorie Casebier McCoy, in her book *To Die With Style!*, quotes suicide and *thanatology* expert Dr. Edwin Shneidman, who describes an *appropriate* death as *one that permits a person to die in a way that is better than the way he would have died if he hadn't seen where he was in the flow of things*. I suggest you are more likely to die an *appropriate death*, and one with dignity, if you are

- aware you're approaching your death and can accept it

- surrounded by loving family and friends during your last days

- given permission to die by those you count most important

- free from chemicals or machines that needlessly prolong life

- able to die peacefully, whether conscious or medicated

- treated with pain control and hospice care, if needed

- can deepen your love relationships and say your goodbyes

If your physicians diagnose you to be terminally ill and prescribe certain medications and treatments, your attempt to die with dignity will include asking them to be honest with you about their odds of extending your days and helping you maintain a satisfying quality of life. You will want this information to compare it with the promise of alternative treatment and of no treatment at all. You have a right to know how your doctors measure success and what your chances are of achieving it. Getting truth from your doctor can save you from feeling disconnected from reality and suffering unnecessarily. You do not want to live your last days under false pretenses—either your doctors' or your own—and die in the dark.

Getting the truth at this point may not be easy, however. Ambiguity, uncertainty, and unpredictability almost always darken these questions and they're not usually resolved easily. Medicine is not an exact science. Asking your doctors for the truth can create tension because they may be focused on defeating the medical problem rather than making your last days as comfortable and satisfying as possible. They are also terrified of being accused of having taken away the last vestiges of their patients' hope and of not having done everything they could to keep them alive. All of this is understandable. But if you end up disagreeing with your doctor or you don't know what to do about the fact you are dying, you can contact a local hospice program for help.

Hospices support patients and their families when doctors determine that a terminally ill patient has less than six months to live. Hospice care does not work to prolong or shorten life, but aims to provide individualized care, ordinarily in the patient's home. It's an interdisciplinary service with specially trained doctors and nurses who focus not on a cure but on maximizing comfort and quality of life for the patient. According to the National Hospice and Palliative Care Organization, in 2010, over four thousand, four hundred hospice programs served an estimated one million, one hundred thousand patients in the United States, about one in three Americans who died in that year.

It's important to see that dying with dignity means having some say about what happens in your last days. Most of the time, anyone but the person who is dying controls what happens; it's usually medical personnel, lawyers, HMO or insurance representatives, financial counselors, professional caregivers, other strangers, and family members. Sometimes that's necessary, at least in part, but we know that others may not be able to fulfill all of our wishes. What we can insist on, however, is that they take our wishes seriously. No matter how caring your doctors or family mean to be as you approach your last days, if you believe they are dismissing your wishes, it will be hard for you to attach much dignity to your dying.

Some people don't have their wishes carried out because they don't make them known. There is no guarantee that you'll get what you want with regard to your dying, but if you think it through and then spell it out to loved ones and your doctors, you will increase the probability. As I noted earlier, it is to your benefit to talk about your dying with those most important to you and to record your specific wishes in a living will or living trust. The time to do that and to become informed about hospice services in your community is now.

I have watched many people go through a prolonged stage two. Some, stunned by their prognosis, overwhelmed by possible complications, and worried about whether they will ever get back to work or feel like themselves, act as victims. Rather than seeking counseling, some become depressed and withdraw. Others, with length of life as their only concern, spend their last months searching frantically for magical cures for their diseases, sometimes submitting to bizarre and desperate treatments. A few manage to temporarily stave off their dying, but usually the quality of their lives fades badly.

I've also witnessed others who, after carefully weighing quality-of-life issues, treat this stage of their dying as a time to decide which treatments they will and will not undergo. Some even try to determine when and how they will die. Making these decisions is seldom easy and is unique to every person. For one thing, the quality of the life you can expect is difficult to measure—especially when you are on various medications or undergoing chemotherapy or other serious treatment. Changes are unpredictable, and the risks are hard to calculate. Because the instinct to live is so powerful, those who have been told they have a specific, limited time often find they will settle for a lower quality of life than they thought they would when dying wasn't imminent.

The controversial Oregon assisted suicide program has shown that such change of heart is common. In the first seven years of the program, during which the state permitted doctors to administer lethal drugs to the terminally ill, only about one in a thousand qualified patients opted to die that way. Supporters of the program point out that what is important is that the law grants them the dignity of *making the choice*. They argue that when citizens' choose to die is not the state's business.

Theologian Jurgen Moltmann contends that just as life and love are an art, *the ability to die is also an art*. Some people who are told they have limited weeks or months to live and who are fairly alert see their last days as an opportune time to deepen bonds with and enjoy family and friends. They become artists in Moltmann's sense—they make their dying as beautiful an adventure as they can, which, in many cases, enriches both themselves and their loved ones.

Three longtime friends of mine who dealt creatively with their last days stand out in my mind. Barbara and I knew Marilyn for almost forty years. She was divorced and in her mid-sixties in the 1990s. She never smoked but was raised in a home with a chain-smoking father and suffered from smoke-induced lung cancer that spread widely. After months of bravely fighting her disease alone in her home in Sacramento, she accepted an invitation from her daughter, Dana, to live in her guest room in Oakland. As her need for painkillers increased and it became clear that she might not have long to live, Dana invited her mother's friends to visit two and three at a time for intimate conversation and tea. We went to see her. Visitors usually listened, held her hand, and whispered loving goodbyes. We shared tears, but Marilyn obviously felt surrounded by love. The scene was filled with dignity and serenity.

Early in the new millennium, our seventy-year-old friend Stan was dying of cancer in Houston, Texas. When told he had less than six months to live, he opted for home hospice care. A parade of friends came to visit daily, openly conceding to the impending death and sharing old stories, expressions of love, fond memories, tears, and laughter. Relieved by pain medications, he held court for a couple of months from a bed in his living room before lapsing into a coma shortly before he died.

Barbara and I knew Stan and his wife, Doris, from college, through seminary days, and during our first calls to ministry together in Orlando, Florida. We celebrated our twenty-fifth wedding anniversaries together. When we heard that his end was near, we flew to Houston to be with him, Doris, and their two children, Beth and Tim. We arrived at their home a couple of days before Stan lapsed into the coma. In his last hours awake, we reminisced about our half-century of friendship. He thanked us for being there and told us how much his family and the visits of friends had meant to him.

Also early in the new millennium, my good friend, Norm, was afflicted by myelofibrosis. This rare, incurable, debilitating disease attacks the bone marrow that produces red blood cells. Norm and I first met on our college basketball court and quickly bonded. Upon graduation, along with his brothers, I was a groomsman at his wedding to Enid. Two months later, when I married Barbara, he was my best man. Over the next several decades, when both of us were actively serving as Presbyterian ministers, he was a colleague and confidante. For a half century, he was the brother I never had. He believed in life and love, and I loved and respected him deeply.

As Norm's strength receded and conventional treatments proved inadequate, he decided to *roll the dice* (his own words)—he would undergo a new and promising experimental stem cell treatment at the highly respected University of California Medical Center in San Francisco. Sadly, it didn't work. During his last year, he deteriorated steadily, despite the treatments and loving care from Enid. All the while, he kept his faith and his marvelous sense of humor. When friends asked how he was doing, he'd reply, *I'm doing great... except for this fatal illness I have.*

As it became clear that Norm had only weeks or days to live, Enid gathered their kids, Emily, Steve, Carol, and Aaron, and the three grandchildren at the family home. Emily and her family came from Great Britain. They spent days reviewing family albums and videos with Norm. Through it all, they hugged and kissed, wept and laughed. Together they make cremation arrangements and Norm helped plan his memorial services. Though both the disease and the treatments were painful and physically debasing, family and friends surrounded Norm with love, and he obviously savored his last hours.

The last days for Marilyn, Stan, and Norm were times of dignity because their families accepted the inevitability and naturalness of the impending death, gave their loved ones the room to be themselves, respected their wishes, and communicated not only their pain but also their genuine gratitude for the life they were about to lose. As a result, not only were they all drawn closer together, but their shared grief through the third stage of dying became beautiful and enriching. They all experienced what I believe is a *good death*.

It's important to know that good deaths don't elicit only positive feelings; those left behind often find themselves with mixed feelings about what they have gone through. They may be sad about their loss while relieved that their loved one's suffering is over. If they're elated that the burden of caring for the deceased is ended, they may feel guilty about it. They also may be troubled by the prospect of a profound loneliness. Even the best of deaths can involve mourning as well as celebrating, eliciting tears as well as expressed gratitude and the sharing of warm memories. In any case, each of us has just one death to die, and I'm suggesting that a *good* death is preferable to a *bad* death.

It may have occurred to you that taking care of business and dying with dignity does not sound like the admonition Welsh poet Dylan Thomas gives his elderly father in one of his best-known poems. The old man has been his son's model of robust strength, but he falls ill and is frail and near to death. Thomas beseeches him: *Do not go gentle into that good night... Rage, rage against the dying of the light.* We can all appreciate the poet's pain and anger at his father's sure descent toward death, but I'm not sure that raging does that much good. *Dying with dignity* doesn't call for you to be passive or benign in the face of death, but it asks you to move past the anger and kind of rage Thomas spoke of, to some measure of acceptance.

When thinking about dying with dignity, we may benefit from reflecting on the most famous death in Western history, even though its circumstances were extraordinary, to say the least. If you want to review the accounts firsthand, you can find them toward the end of each of the four Gospels at the beginning of the New Testament in the Christian Bible.

Jesus' dying is different in the extreme from what you and I are likely to experience and, at first glance, the opposite of dying with dignity. When brutal Roman authorities crucify him, he is in his prime—his early thirties. Crucifixion is the epitome of cruel and unusual punishment. Soldiers drive crude spikes through his hands and feet, plunge a spear into his side, and leave him to hang on a cross for hours. When Jesus cries from thirst, his tormentors mock him, pressing a bitter, vinegar-soaked sponge to his lips.

It may strike you as crazy to think of Jesus' death as good, but several things the Gospel writers say he said and did in his last hours typify dying with dignity. On the night he is betrayed—that is, the night before he is put to death—he eats with his disciples—his most intimate extended family—what Christians call the Last Supper, during which he takes care of some unfinished personal business. Later that night, in the Garden of Gethsemane, while agonizing over the near certain prospect of his impending death, he prays to be spared from it, if possible (he knows there will be unbearable suffering to endure, and there is work still to be done). At the same time, he strongly affirms that the righteous will of his God in pursuit of peace with justice is more important than what he is asking. He obviously believes that the purposes for which he has lived and is about to die are larger than he is. He also gives us reason to believe he has no regrets and has come to terms with his dying despite his young age and the injustice of it all.

The next afternoon, while being tormented on the cross, he turns the care of his mother over to his best friend, John, and, incredibly, he publicly forgives his false accusers and the executioners. He also utters two final statements that are highly significant. In the first, he says, *Father, I put myself in your hands.* As he faces the end, he bets on *agape.* He hands his life over to the grace and mercy he found at the foundation and center of life—the profound and powerful sense of compassion and justice that drew him to his mission, that helped him create his best possible life and that now helps him die in peace.

In his final statement, he cries, *It is finished!* Some biblical scholars say Jesus was expressing his belief that he had completed what he felt was the unique task his God had called him to do. Others see it as the final word of a man who had lived for, and was about to die for, the noble values of truth, justice, and liberation for his oppressed people. Still others think he simply was saying he knew his life and suffering were about to end. Whatever interpretation we choose, we have no reason to believe that Jesus died burdened with disturbing fear or regret. Despite the torture and unjust execution he suffered, we can say that his death was as good as his remarkable life.

What does your heart ask of you as to how you will die?

What does how you live say about your chance for dying well?

What can you do today to enhance your dying tomorrow?

Approach Six: Wrestle with the Ultimate Mystery

Since the dawn of human consciousness we have faced our existence as mystery. Only the most curious among us, however, have been fascinated by and spent time pondering such large, philosophical questions as why anything exists rather than nothing; when and why the universe came to be; what else other than our universe can be said to be real; when life itself started; and why our brain evolved to the point that we alone—of all the beings of which we're aware—began to conceive and seek answers to such questions. Perhaps most of us don't struggle with these questions, because we think any answers we might find will have little effect on our personal lives.

But we all face what I refer to here as the awesome, intimate, *ultimate mystery*—that is, what happens to you and me as persons in death, the state, or non-state of being we enter when we die. And while it's mainly the most religious who spend serious time occupied with it, I suggest it's important for all of us to think about, because any theory we choose can affect our lives, and because at least 75 percent of Americans believe we as individuals will live on in a never-ending afterlife. It's the view held by most Christians and Muslims, some Jews, and a lot of otherwise secular people. Some insist that *where you will spend eternity* (your existence after you die) is the most important question for which you need the correct, true answer, and, if you find it you will wound, if not kill, the grim reaper. Whether or not we think an *afterlife* refers to anything real, the wide affirmation of this belief makes it something we all owe it to ourselves to give some thought.

Those who have spent two seconds thinking about what happens when we die tend to hold one of seven views. Here they are in a nutshell:

1. **Extinction**: Skeptics, old and new atheists, and other hard-core secularists contend that when your heart stops pumping blood to your brain and shuts down, your body decays, the *light* in you that people refer to as soul or spirit goes out, and you cease to exist. You are dead and gone. End of story.

2. **An Unknowable Mystery**: Agnostics say that almost any claim about the existence of an afterlife may or may not be true to some degree and in some form. They figure that when you die, you may become extinct or undergo an experience different from and perhaps far more mind-boggling than anything you or I can imagine. Until then, they say, there is no way to know what to expect. When asked about an afterlife, agnostics answer, *I don't know.*

3. **The Ongoing Impact of Your Relationships and Creations**: Through your influence and others' memories, you remain alive in those persons you touched for good or for ill. You may

also live on through tangible contributions you make to culture and human understanding. In this way, ahead of time, you enjoy a secular form of *afterlife*. (This is the immortality Woody Allen is not keen on.)

4. **The Immortality of the Soul:** Many ancient peoples, including Zoroastrian Persians and philosophical Greeks, held this view. They wished to be like the gods, who they believed possessed everlasting life, although they had no assurance it could happen to them. They concluded that when we die, the physical body rots, but the spiritual self (the soul or spirit), no longer having a body to inhabit, loses its particular identity and melds into an eternal spirit, or absolute soul, like a drop of rainwater joins the sea.

5. **Reincarnation:** This theory from ancient India, taught mainly by Eastern philosophers, holds that animals and humans live many lives and go through many deaths, repeatedly returning to earth in bodily form, or *incarnation*, human or otherwise. It portrays all of us as participating in a *never-ending recycling program* or a great spiritual evolutionary process, working forever toward perfection through many incarnations.

6. **The Metaphysical/Spirit World:** Death leads to the *beyond*, or *the other side*, in which the physical part of us has no place. This is an afterlife known to psychics, clairvoyants, and other mystics, so they say. They know of this world because *spirit guides* who live there have visited them, they have seen this world on the *astral screens* of their minds, and they transport messages from the spirits of the dead to the living. It's the realm generally reported on by those who have had near-death experiences—persons who got their foot in the door and were sent back. They say it is more beautiful than we are able to imagine.

7. **Resurrection of the Body:** Most Christians say that if you trust Jesus and love and worship God, upon death you will go

with your same consciousness and identity to heaven above to be forever with Jesus, God, your loved ones, and others who believed in Jesus. Another Christian view says that if you are a believer your spirit stays with your body in the grave, as if you are asleep. Then, when Jesus comes back to bring down the curtain of history, you will be resurrected to meet him in the sky and be taken off to heaven. Both schemes insist there is life after death. If you don't trust in Jesus and fail to love God and meet his requirements, your body will rot and you will join all the other godless, unbelieving sinners in hell.

Theories five, six and seven affirm some kind of ongoing existence with your personal consciousness and identity intact. These theories capture the minds of most Americans for several reasons:

- The scales of justice do not balance in this life (children starve, the righteous suffer, those who act wickedly get richer), and our sense of a *final good* goes unsatisfied. If morality and the dignity or sacredness of our humanity are to make sense, things must even out—evil must be punished and good vindicated. The doctrine of hell, which I talked about earlier, and the Roman Catholic idea of purgatory seek to satisfy this inherent and universal sense of justice that tells us we violate something of *ultimate* significance when we fail to respect the rights of others, and we should be punished.

- Existing as living, breathing creatures is what we know. When faced with the thought of *nonbeing*—that is, of not existing after we die, our life instinct and love of life feel violated. This idea so depresses and frightens some of us that we unconsciously choose to believe in some form of personal immortality. Such fear and depression seems to be common, even though, as far as I know, none of us is bothered by *not being* before we were born. This lack of anxiety seems akin to what Cicero was referring to in 45 BC when he said, *I don't want to die, but I wouldn't care if I were dead.*

- Uniquely among all the species on Earth, humans are able to *imagine* the eternal and the infinite, even if we can't *comprehend* them. This convinces some people that we've been created—or that evolution has designed us—to live forever, and that despite the death of the physical brain it makes sense in some way that human consciousness, mind, spirit, or soul may evolve or be transformed and survive.

- Some people cannot shake what William Wordsworth called *intimations of immortality*—inexplicable nonphysical signs that seem to point beyond material reality to an *eternal now*, a primitive life force, or a mysterious, spiritual life that exists on a higher plane. Some believe that the universal desire for love and peace with justice, lit by imagination and hope, signals a truth greater than what can be found in matter. They may also think in terms of the possible existence of consciousness beyond the one we now know, perhaps within the different dimensions of what scientists conceive of as parallel universes, though not necessarily supernatural or spooky ones.

- The dramatic Christian story of Jesus' resurrection and the promise of an everlasting life of bliss to unwavering believers, faithful church goers, the doctrinally correct, the baptized, really good people, and martyrs or saints—depending on which church you listen to—sits deeply in our American mind and elicits powerful emotional attachments. They see the resurrection of Jesus as evidence of life after death and a decisive blow to the power of death. It caused St. Paul in I Corinthians, Chapter 15, to quote an ancient poem,

Death is swallowed up in victory. O death, where is thy victory?
O death, where is thy sting?
(Revised Standard Version)

While surveys show that the percentage of Christians who believe in heaven is on the decline, a good majority of Americans still say they believe that life on earth is not, or ought not to be all there is. Most believe in some form of ongoing existence after death. For some, it's a way of saying, *Take that, grim reaper!* They see it as a matter of anesthetizing the sting, or of defeating the ultimate threat of death. Many admit they believe in a blissful afterlife because they were taught to believe in it as children, it makes them feel better, and it's what they hope is true. Believe what you will, but I contend it's important to remember, that a belief's longevity and popularity, and wishful thinking and certainty have never been sure signs of truth.

If the notion of an afterlife comes easily to you, look at several problems it increasingly presents to informed, thinking persons. First, believers need to recognize they possess no hard evidence to support their certainty about life after death. We're aware that the ancient world was filled with reports of special persons who rose from the grave, including Jesus. We also know that understandings of the nature of the universe and our humanity before modern science arose were fraught with superstition, and misinformation. Believers do have reasons for their convictions, but just as skeptics cannot offer demonstrable proof that God and heaven do not exist, believers cannot prove the opposite. They must admit that belief boils down to calculated choice. Might the ultimate irony be that those who desperately want to go to heaven will do everything they can to avoid dying?

Another problem with belief in life after death is that it produces mixed moral results in the behavior of believers. For good, it consoles and inspires oppressed, downtrodden, and unlucky people who have no hope of a dignified and pleasurable life here and now. But it also causes people to be so preoccupied with life after death they get derailed and fail to contribute to the common good; they are, as the old saying goes, *so heavenly minded, they are no earthly good at all.* Also, while the promise of a beautiful afterlife leads many to die for country, faith, family, and their God—sacrifices most people consider noble—it also compels religious fanatics to callously kill children and other innocents to get some kind of heavenly reward.

A third problem is that most believers take the notion of heaven without much thought and give the impression they are frightened of having skeptics challenge it. They cut themselves off from those who ask hard questions of their faith, questions for which they know they don't have answers that will hold water with informed, thinking people. They may have reasons for their belief, but when confronted with facts they finally insist that their critics will have to *take it on faith*. If their avoidance is akin to *whistling in the dark*, perhaps it's a matter of not wanting their *whistling* interrupted or drowned out. At the least, they appear to be more interested in security and personal comfort than in the truth.

World-renowned British physicist Stephen Hawking says he believes that heaven is nothing more than *a fairy story* invented by people who are *afraid of the dark* … A British newspaper quotes Hawking as saying, *I regard the brain as a computer which will stop working when its components fail. There is no heaven or afterlife for broken-down computers.* A scientific-thinking friend of mine, Richard Golden, says, *If it is my personality that's to be preserved after my death, my memories must also be preserved. But my memories are stuck in my brain, and after death my brain will have turned to mush.* The world's best neurobiologists, almost without exception, say the same thing.

It may be true there are scientists who are not convinced our identities and memories are stuck in the brain, but if you claim certainty about a heavenly afterlife, I suggest you owe it to yourself and to your faith to wrestle with such a claim and attempt to answer other troubling (including perhaps humorous) questions posed by disbelievers:

When you're in heaven, what age will you be?

Will children who die here be adults there?

If you can't choose what you'll be or do, how appealing is that?

118

What will your spiritual body be like?

Will you have tight abs, no wrinkles, look like a million dollars?

Will you be stuck wearing the clothes you were buried in?

If you are blown to bits or cremated, how will you be resurrected?

Who will you spend eternity with, and do you have a choice?

If your parents or siblings abused you at one time, but later got religion, would you like to spend eternity with them?

How about your pet? If there are no dogs in heaven, Will Rogers said, *then when I die I want to go where they went.*

What if you hear heaven is like an endless church service?

Suppose heaven is where humans become sexless winged creatures that endlessly play harps. Would you want to go near such a place?

If you leave your weaknesses behind, how can you still be you?

Apropos of this last question, the April 12, 2010, issue of *The New Yorker* magazine bears a cartoon showing St. Peter checking a man in at the gate, saying, *No, sorry, you'll still be dumb.* If this were true of the afterlife, we all might ask whether God should apologize for making us the way we are.

Many thoughtful people who ponder a never-ending existence are appalled by what it might be like. Edgar Shoaff thinks it sounds like a *fate worse than death.* The late San Francisco columnist Herb Caen believed that the only thing wrong with immortality is that *it tends to go on forever.* Playwright Tom Stoppard bemoans eternity as a terrible thought, asking, *where is it all going to end?* Mark Twain thought it all sounds *so boring.* Susan Ertz noted (before TV) that *millions long for immortality who don't know what to do on a rainy afternoon.* I suppose they all wonder what we would do with all that time.

Heaven's cosmic geography creates another problem for the traditional Christian view of life after death. Almost all believers before the twentieth century interpreted everything in the Bible as historical fact. They took literally the Gospel writers' reports that Jesus not only was crucified, died, and was buried but that he also was bodily resurrected, left his tomb empty, and floated physically up through the clouds to heaven, where he sat down and still sits on a throne at his father's right hand. From there, they believe, he will return one day to put an end to time, swooping down from beyond the clouds with angels to a blast of trumpets, meeting both alive and long-dead believers rising from their graves and taking them to heaven to be forever with God. As noted earlier, nonbelievers will be *left behind* and sent to hell to be with the fallen angel Lucifer and suffer their due eternal punishment of hellfire and damnation. This biblical view—certainly not shared by all Christians–ties all these events together and claims they outline God's great plan for his earthly, mortal children.

With the spread of higher education in the sciences and liberal arts during the last half of the twentieth century, the three-deck universe of times past collapsed for informed, thinking people, including many Christians. We now know that the universe and our planet are nothing like what the ancients imagined them to be. No self-aware, thoughtful believer can still speak of (1) a blissful heaven up in the sky someplace where God and Jesus abide, (2) the Earth in the middle where we live, and (3) a Dante-depicted cauldron of eternal fire pits down below in the basement, the dwelling place of Satan and his evil demons. Yet Christian fundamentalists, evangelicals, and sentimentalists—maybe half of all Americans—still take these images literally; and many of them have one eye cocked toward the sky. What are they thinking? Are they thinking at all?

Because the images associated with the heaven and hell perpetuated by the church tend to be cute and funny, even silly, cartoonists and joke tellers continue to use them—St. Peter at the pearly gates, winged angels on clouds playing harps, horned demons wearing red suits stoking coals of fire with pitchforks, and so on. But, again, while we live in the supposedly enlightened twenty-first century, a significant percentage of Americans believe these images represent what we will face after we die.

The world recognizes the late Joseph Campbell as the foremost authority on mythology. In a famous 1988 PBS television series called *The Power of Myth*, Campbell stresses the universality and evolution of myth in the history of the human race. Among other things, he notes that the idea of resurrection is found in virtually all cultures, in addition to the three great monolithic religions. In this sense, myths are not history, but tales with dramatic symbols and personages put together to help us grasp profound truths much deeper than what we see on the surface. Historically we humans have always created myths to help hold life and death together.

Thoughtful Christians who want to rid their faith of superstition, fantasy, and *cockeyed* views of reality are fond of saying they take the Bible *seriously* but not *literally*. They approach it as they do other ancient texts, treating biblical law as law, history as history, poetry as poetry, prophecy as prophecy, proverbs as proverbs, allegory as allegory, and, certainly, myth as myth. They see Jesus' resurrection, ascension, and second coming as mythological. They are not historical events but symbolic acts that emerge from and reflect a radical change in the minds of his disciples, or closest followers. When Roman authorities crucify him, his disciples must go on without him in a world defined by cruel violence, political oppression, abject poverty, suffering and death. As they do, his compelling vision of peace with justice imprints itself on their hearts and, coupled with the power of their new commitment to nonviolently resist oppressors, resurrects them from despair to hope. What he had to say and who he became to them so touches their hearts and minds, they become willing, as Jesus had been, not to kill but to live and die for what his transcendent truths about love mean to them, their children, and their trampled, occupied nation.

Most biblical scholars conclude that the authors of the New Testament adopted the mythical, apocalyptic imagery of their predecessors in ancient

Zoroastrianism and Judaism. They believe Jesus' followers drew upon such dramatic imagery to say that with his messages about economic and social justice, nonviolent resistance to evil, compassion for the poor, being narrow-minded about broadmindedness, and radical forgiveness for everyone, including one's enemies, Jesus nailed what it takes to revitalize and sustain the world community. They were trying to say that he took on all the powers of destruction and revealed the deepest, redemptive truths about our existence, rooting them in *agape*. They also were convinced, rightly or naively, that the die is cast—the truth of his teachings will one day ring true to the entire human family and determine its redemption.

It is interesting and important to note that the faith of the writers of the four Gospels didn't *transport* them to another world but *transformed* them for this one. Biblical scholars tell us that Jesus' oft-used phrase the *kingdom of heaven*—interchangeable with the *kingdom of God*, is not a place you go after you die. The political term *kingdom*, stands for *reign* or *rule* in the social order, not a *realm*. It speaks of the power of *agape* to shape a just and compassionate society, and it says you experience heaven when this love shapes the worlds you live in, and when you can receive and give love. And eternal life refers to earthly experiences nourished by and lived under the power of this perfect love that is unbounded by time and space.

Accordingly, the scholars I mention above see hell as the opposite of heaven, as human society dominated by injustice, oppression, and violence. It is the experience of not being loved, not being able to love or to commit to the worthwhile human purposes that love generates, and, perhaps most of all, not being able to know and love who you are. As with heaven, they say, we go through hell right here and now.

These Christians call *sadistic nonsense* the notion that the God of Jesus would send nonbelievers to everlasting torture when they die. They believe that because *agape* stands over all other powers, no one need worry about being eternally punished for their shortcomings, weaknesses and failures, what the church historically has called *sin*. Yes, we all, including the most evil among us, have a right to fear needless physical suffering during the third and fourth stages of dying. And those who intentionally continue to violate the law of love and abuse others should be terrified of never finding inner peace and joy. But because *agape* is the overarching truth about us, the *glue that holds human life together,* the first and final word that defines our human experience—even the worst of us need not worry about what will happen to us after we die.

Another problem with belief in life-after-death arises because Christian evangelicals and fundamentalists, its chief proponents, demean us and the dignity of our existence by making life's primary goal the avoidance of hell. They peddle, as it were, the ultimate *fire insurance.* They say you will escape the eternal fires if you do what they say their God requires of you. If you believe them and are obedient, God will open the door to heaven for you. If you fail to meet God's requirements, the door stays shut, and you go to hell. This life is God's test, a trial. You either pass or fail.

This view divides the human family into believers and infidels, accepted and rejected, *saved* and *unsaved.* It's based on archaic ideas of a vengeful God who treats his trusting children to eternal bliss but punishes his wayward off-spring by seeing they burn forever. You are one of the saved and will go to heaven or you're one of the unsaved, bound for the fires of eternal damnation.

This insidious dividing of the human family makes the saved feel right-eous, superior, and safe; those they designate the unsaved feel inferior and abandoned by the saved and by God. The saved say they love the unsaved. In reality, they don't; they look on them as persons toward whom they can feel pity, and as objects to manipulate and convert. They accept and affirm them only if they say *yes* to being converted; if they say *no,* the saved sooner or later ignore and discard them. This patronizing division strikes me as a perverse betrayal of Jesus' *agape.* Church history reeks with the shame of terrible theology, but is it any wonder in this day and age that intelligent, thoughtful Christians are appalled and embarrassed by this way of seeing history and of treating non-Christians? And does it surprise us that John Lennon calls us to *imagine* a world that doesn't include a heaven, a hell, and religion?

Lest I seem to have treated Jesus' resurrection cavalierly and *needlessly* offend some Christians, let me note that a wide range of highly respected scholars, including some who have no vested interest in Christian doctrine, find significant meaning in the symbolic images of *death, resurrection, ascension,* and *return*. They have produced interpretations of *resurrection as internal transformation* far more nuanced than what I've described here. Unfortunately, the vast cultural divide from the ancient world, the academic jargon of scholars, and the Church's tendency to censor interpretations that challenge its historic doctrine make the ideas of these scholars mostly inaccessible to the vast majority of ordinary people.

Also, many of the kinds of philosophical mysteries I mentioned earlier—why there is something rather than nothing, why life itself began, and so on—refuse to yield to scientific and rational analysis. So do such notions as unconditional and sacrificial love, infinity, eternity, and the paradox of losing your life in order to find it. It's good to keep in mind that the opposite of *rational* is not always *irrational or anti-rational,* sometimes it's *transrational,* which means it deals in realities the rational mind simply cannot process. Perhaps any rational repugnance to such ideas as transcendent spirit and an ongoing afterlife might be due to the limits of rationality and our own meager imaginations. It's a thought.

When it comes to what happens to us individually after we die, I join those who lean on this mystery of *agape*. We believe that while we all fall short of what others reasonably expect of us and of what we expect of ourselves, this transcendent love accepts us all, despite our flaws. In other words, no one will be devalued or lost forever. More importantly, we try to live compassionate, just, and truthful lives not to pass any test, or to appease an angry, judgmental God, or to earn a reward when this life is over, but to respond appropriately to life as a gift and enjoy our best possible lives.

I stressed earlier that living gains worthwhile meaning when we face our dying, for it makes each moment we have infinitely valuable. I also said that *agape,* the defining love that was here before we arrived, is *the ground and heart of being itself,* so to live our best life we must choose to love in this way. Isn't it clear that this love supplies what we need to live fully and that in one sense, *all you need is love?* It is to me. I suggest it is the only power worthy of our unquestioning trust and undying loyalty, not only because it is what first and finally enriches our life but also because to be loved and to know it can take the sting from the mystery of what happens after we die.

I don't think we can know what death will mean to us in the same way we now know that the earth revolves around the sun. On the question of immortality, I'm essentially agnostic, although I love life and retain a measure of hope that we yet may find something that both fits the facts of what we know about our existence and honors human dignity. In any case, the issue of the afterlife is not of major concern to me. When discussing it with my longtime friend Dorothy, she confides, *If when I die it's like being asleep, or if it's a wonderful new existence, either way, it'll be okay.* I feel the same way.

A few years back, I led memorial services for a couple who died eleven months apart. On the bulletin covers at each gathering they had arranged for the same statement to appear:

> *When you come to the edge of all the light you have;*
> *And you must take a step into the darkness of the unknown,*
> *Either there will be something solid for you to stand on, or you will fly.*

When we put our trust in the perfect love of *agape* and step into that ultimate unknown, we have solid ground to stand on (*you are accepted!*) and the freedom to fly (*you can be yourself!*). So again I leave the question of afterlife in the hands of love and mystery and I don't spend one minute worrying about it.

Whatever you believe about any kind of afterlife, it may help to realize that not one of the seven theories I described is backed by indisputable evidence. Perhaps this alone will keep you humble, tolerant, and searching for clarity of insight as you reconstruct your worldview and take steps toward achieving your best possible life.

Final Thoughts on the Ultimate Mystery

At the center of our life lies a deep anxiety generated by an awareness that like all members of the other species we will one day die. In attempting to smother this angst, we tend to do the exact opposite of what we need to do. We allow false pride and wishful thinking to paint portraits in our imagination not of what we are and of what is but of what we like to think we are and of what we hope will be. Deep down, we know we're mortal, but we suppress that knowledge and conjure in our minds the idea that death cannot or will not touch us. Then, when we draw near to dying, we find ourselves shaken and inept. We may try to project an image to others that tells them we're strong, we're *cool*, and we're not afraid of dying, but because this distorted projection contradicts and denies two truths central to our living—that is, that we are both mortal and anxious—it's hard for us not only to face our dying but also to live our best possible life.

Fortunately, great minds have provided lights along the way to help us see truer pictures of ourselves and paths to authenticity and our best possible lives. We have looked at a number of them. In part one, I laid out ten steps you can take to strengthen your worldview and your ability to live your best possible life. In part two, I have described six approaches to your dying that will help you deal with both your life and your death more creatively:

1. Accept your eventual dying as inevitable.

2. View your dying as part of a natural process.

3. Face your fears.

4. Vow to Die with minimum regret.

5. Prepare to die with dignity.

6. Wrestle with the ultimate mystery.

It is important for you to know that one day you will die and to learn about healthy approaches to your dying. But it isn't enough. Others may light your path with truth, but to control what you can of your own journey and to live your best possible life, you must take your own steps. The task is to act on your new understandings of living and dying. Death is the most noted certainty in life and your clock is running. This means that the tendency to put important matters on the back burner is your worst enemy.

Humorist P. J. O'Rourke thinks you should always read *stuff that will make you look good if you die in the middle of it.* You've almost completed this book, and I hope you've found it to be that kind of *stuff.* At the least, I trust that what you have read here has been helpful and that you will not die before you read the two very personal postscripts that follow.

At the most, I wish you a long, good life at your best; and peace at the last.

When Life Ends

For sainted, a gentle crossing;
Surrounded by love.
Fragile, still clinging to life.
Inevitable fate, courage,
Bravely, bravely smiling.
Knowing the end is near.
Slowly drifting into that deep sleep,
With Saintly serenity,
A good soul departing.
An unknown journey
Only Barbara will decide,
And she decided.

The body is gone,
Pictures remain on the wall,
You are still here.

Ben Slomoff   October 27, 2008

We all know we're going to die. What's important is the kind of men and women we are in the face of this.

Anne Lamott

Perhaps the love we have given and received is the energy that lives on when our dust returns to the earth and our atoms merge with the rest of creation.

Majorie Casebier McCoy

Grief turns out to be a place none of us know until we reach it. We anticipate (we know) that someone close to us could die, but we do not look beyond the few days or weeks that immediately follow such an imagined death.

Joan Didion

All I know is that I must soon die, but what I know least is this very death that I cannot escape.

Blaise Pascal

PERSONAL POSTSCRIPT ONE

I stand by my six approaches to dying and death, but I'm aware that words can be cheap when writing to strangers about *their* eventual dying. I know it's a lot easier than facing the dying of someone close to me, or my own.

In these postscripts, written in the spring of 2011, I describe two intimate, recent brushes with my mortality. I write to help you grasp not only their significance for me but also for you. I start with the dying of Barbara, my beloved wife of fifty-four years, in October 2008.

What I hear of Barbara Hargreaves when we both are teenagers in different schools near Philadelphia grabs my attention. When I finally meet her, I discover what all the fuss is about. She is smart, a star athlete, and beautiful. I would later say that the actress, and then-princess, Grace Kelly, looks like Barbara Hargreaves.

Teammates elect her captain of her high school field hockey, basketball and tennis teams. She is voted best athlete and best looking in her senior class and wins the female scholar-athlete award (she is something special, no?). From high school, she goes off to nurse's training near Chicago. When she reenters my life in my junior year of college, she captures more than my attention. I fall in love (remember that section in part one?). I go after her like gangbusters. She enjoys a lot of attention from other male students, but I sweep her off her feet and lock her up fairly quickly. I often say that I chased her until she caught me.

We tie the knot in August 1954. Working as a nurse, Barbara helps put me through two seminaries in preparation for the Presbyterian ministry. While our four kids are growing up, she gives up nursing for ten years to form strong bonds with them. All the while, I am serving four churches, the last three in the East Bay Area of Northern California. As a minister's wife, with my encouragement, she never becomes other than herself. People love her for her integrity, good values, fitting contributions, and, yes, her beauty as a woman.

If we stop to think for a moment, it's clear that we never really know what other marriages are like, no matter how couples act or what they say in public. With our very different personalities, four strong and independent children, and demanding occupations, Barbara and I survive a couple of difficult times that most people don't know about. Were she here today, she would join me in saying that we deeply loved each other and felt fortunate to have our fifty-four married years together.

In June 1996, Barbara retires after twenty-two years as a nurse for the tough Oakland Unified School District. One year earlier, Time Warner buys my first book, *Too Nice for Your Own Good*. I don't want to miss out on life with Barbara in retirement, so I retire a year early from a rewarding twenty-eight-year pastorate at Oakland's Montclair Presbyterian Church. She continues to volunteer with Amnesty International and the Oakland Museum's White Elephant Sale, and I do the book promotion thing. For exercise and fun, we play more tennis and golf than we did during our child-rearing and hard-working days. Barbara has a 1954 Midwest Intercollegiate Doubles Champion tennis trophy, and I feel privileged to be her partner. I've played golf off and on for forty years, and while she has hardly played at all, for retirement I buy her the necessary equipment and lessons.

In April 2000, we move fifteen miles northeast of Oakland to Rossmoor, an active retirement community of nearly ten thousand residents on the edge of Walnut Creek. Rossmoor sits nestled on the sylvan slopes of the two-and-a-half-mile-long Tice Valley in the shadow of Mt. Diablo, the Bay Area's highest peak. Condominiums cover the hillsides. We find a beautiful spot on Eagle Ridge with privacy and spectacular views of the mountain and settle in to enjoy this splendid community.

Among Rossmoor's amenities and central to the beauty of the valley floor sit twenty-seven holes of golf and a fine set of tennis courts among towering pines and Buckeye oaks. Before long, we are playing tennis and golf together regularly. I work on a couple of books, one of which forms the basis for this one. Barbara continues her work with Amnesty and the Oakland museum.

We maintain close ties with a dozen dear friends, most of whom we've known for half a century. (Because most of them are former ministers, our kids refer to us as the *God Squad*). We also make new friends in Rossmoor. We feel fortunate to have our health, family, great friends, and a wonderful life together.

Eight good years fly by. Life, though mellow, is busy with things we like to do and things we think are important. We are busy with others protesting the Middle East wars outside Rossmoor's entrance every Friday afternoon. We spend family times at Lake Tahoe each summer, take several cruises on which I lecture on my first book, and regularly attend excellent local theater productions. Our kids joke that they practically have to make an appointment to see us. Barbara, who has never worn her feelings on her sleeve, speaks frequently of her pleasure with our life. I tell her I feel the same way. She is essentially at peace with herself, our kids, and me. And so am I.

Late in June 2008, however, she begins to drop things in the kitchen. She's never done anything like this before and doesn't understand why it's happening now. She dismisses it as aging. In early July, at a Saturday tennis club barbecue, she loses her balance and awkwardly bumps into another club member. She's embarrassed and upset and connects it to her recent habit of dropping things. I tell her I want her to check in with our internist that Monday, but she brushes me off and I defer—she is the medical expert in this family.

The next Saturday, we are playing golf with good friends, Richard and Lorrie. Barbara is having a rather mediocre round, which every golfer has at times, and we don't notice anything unusual until we come to the fifth green. She usually putts very well, but in stroking a twenty-footer on level ground, she clumsily punches the ball at a 45-degree angle from the intended line. This puzzles and frightens her—I can see it in her face. Something is obviously wrong and it scares me as well. I say firmly, right there, *We are going to our doctor first thing Monday.* This time she nods, and we finish a bad nine holes.

Early Monday, our doctor suspects Barbara is experiencing side effects from her blood pressure medication. She drafts a new prescription, which we are happy to get filled on our way home. That night, Barbara feels a bit better and we think we have found the answer. The next morning, however, when coincidentally I am scheduled for my annual physical, she feels worse, so I insist she go with me to our doctor. On the way, she says, *I feel like I may be having a stroke.* We arrive early, but I tell the receptionist what Barbara said, and we get right in. Our doctor calls an imaging center across town and arranges a CT brain scan for two-thirty that afternoon.

We arrive at the center a bit early. Barbara submits to the procedure, and when it is finished, the technician asks us to sit in the waiting room. After a few minutes, he comes out and tells us he has notified our doctor that the scan shows *a slight swelling on the right side of her brain.* She wants us to go directly to the emergency room at John Muir Hospital across the street. I feel a blunt blow somewhere deep inside me that says things will never be the same.

In 1993, at age sixty, I had my prostate removed due to a menacing malignant tumor. It was a nasty six weeks and the worst medical crisis either of us had gone through in forty years of marriage. Now in our seventies, we know we can count on facing serious health issues, but because Barbara's been physically active and in such good shape, this news stuns us. She's had some minor back pain and a gradual loss of agility and strength, all of which we associate with aging. But the sudden loss of coordination and this brain-swelling report seem to come from nowhere.

John Muir Hospital is one of just one hundred and fifty-two out of nearly five thousand hospitals across the county that prominently display on their walls framed copies of the *US News & World Report* on hospitals. They all do so, because the magazine ranks them the nation's best. We're glad to have John Muir nearby, but we are anxious as we walk into Admittance.

Once they check Barbara into a private room, we hug and kiss a lot and do some crying in each others' arms. I get the hard news to our daughter, Margo, who lives nearby. She notifies her three brothers. That night, hospital doctors put Barbara through a full body MRI. The next morning, a neurosurgeon explains to Margo and me that they've found more than a *slight swelling of the right side of the brain—five* small tumors are growing there. He tells us it is they that cause the swelling and her loss of coordination, and their number rules out surgery. The scan also reveals a three centimeter malignant tumor in the lower left lung that has metastasized not only to the brain (most brain cancer, we learn, originates somewhere else) but also to the lymph nodes and bone in her back (no doubt the source of that minor back pain she's been feeling). He intimates that with treatment, Barbara may have a year to live, but probably not that long. Margo tears up. We are both a bit numb and my knees shake and threaten to buckle.

From the start, the kids support us in emotional and practical ways. Margo helps me coordinate hospital test schedules. She and our youngest son, Stuart, and his wife, Vicky, who live two hours away in Roseville, bring our six California grandchildren to cram into Grandma's room for a visit. John Muir may not be over it yet, but love surrounds Barbara and she is delighted.

I quickly notify our large contingent of family and friends across the country. Cards, calls, notes, flowers and e-mails pour in from everywhere. At such a harrowing time, these expressions of concern and compassion remind me of what I already know—it must be horrible to face the third and fourth stages of dying without people who love you. I mention this to remind you, if you haven't already done so, to right now make it a priority to *forgive everyone everything*, mend fences, build family, and create loving friendships. In part one, I stressed how important it is to love and be loved every day of your life. Here I want you to see how critical love is when you must face the prospect that your life, or that of someone very close to you, is about to end.

Until her cancer reared its ugly head, Barbara and I had planned to join our children and grandchildren the next week for our annual family time at Lake Tahoe, a twenty-five year tradition. Now in the hospital a few days, we don't know how we can do that. Our doctors know how gravely ill she is and what a short time she has to enjoy her family. Since initial treatments have reduced the swelling in the brain, and Barbara is feeling almost normal, they release her to prepare for radiation and chemotherapy. They also urge us to go first to the lake with family. We go, and spend a bittersweet but wonderful several days there. On Friday I perform a wedding ceremony for Margo and Keld, our new son-in-law. It is an intimate setting on a familiar beach. Keld and I stand at water's edge with our backs to the lake, while Margo and Barbara are beautiful walking down the beach toward us. Our children, grandchildren, and a few close friends surround us. Through our sadness, Barbara glows with love for all of us, and we for her, and she savors every moment. We return home Sunday for a tearful Chinese dinner with the *God Squad*, whom we've not seen since we heard the bad news.

On Tuesday, we are getting with the program; Barbara begins two weeks of *whole-brain* radiation. Our doctors tell us they have a good chance to stave off the worst ravages of the cancer and add to her days and quality of life. We want to believe them. They assure us that if she decides the treatments are worse than the disease, she is free to stop. Barbara the nurse knows she has hard times ahead, but she faces them with courage and some measure of hope.

We live at home, and each morning for two weeks we make the twenty-minute trek across town to the radiation department at John Muir for about a half-hour exposure. Jacqueline, our oldest granddaughter, hearing her grandmother's news, has rushed home from her postgraduate neuroscience studies in Germany. She stands beside us and translates our radiologist's take on the condition of Barbara's brain and her treatment options and plans. We feel fortunate to have her there.

Barbara completes radiation on August 4, about four weeks after our discovery. She experiences a modicum of fatigue, unsteadiness, and nausea but pills take care of them fairly quickly. Tests show that, as expected, the brain swelling has further receded. Because she has generally good health, strong family support, and a positive yet realistic outlook in her favor, our oncologist encourages her to fight the cancer with chemotherapy. Barbara agrees. The doctor schedules six three-hour chemo treatments, each of them three weeks apart.

We more or less have gained our bearings and are executing a plan, but we also have been in this *twilight zone* long enough to know that curves can be thrown at us at any time. We find traipsing back and forth to the hospital, the lab, and various doctors' offices relatively easy. What isn't easy is dealing with the constant changes in Barbara's multiple doses of medicines. I keep a computer file on her meds by dosage, time, purpose, doctor's name, etc. and fax it to all of her doctors every time one of them changes something. We spend a good bit of time checking to make sure we are all on the same page. Summer vacations and replacement people make communication tricky. We've created no disasters, but as I close my eyes for sleep each night, I'm always afraid one might be lurking in the darkness.

On July 31, so they don't have to keep jabbing Barbara's veins, a surgeon implants a port into her chest to facilitate the chemo infusions. Every three weeks for several months—or until she decides not to—she will spend three hours having the prescribed toxic substance pumped into her bloodstream. Our oncologist tells us that for a few days, it is normal for patients to feel sick.

Barbara eagerly takes this on. I am both amazed and unsurprised by her courage. A week after the first treatment, however, she is feeling so miserable that she says, *I don't want any more chemo.* It is no glib comment; I can see in her face how terrible she feels, and it breaks my heart. I reaffirm with her that we will honor whatever she decides to do. Even as I say this, I realize I am placing a terrible burden on her—in the midst of her staggering grief, I am asking her alone to decide her destiny. I worry whether this does her a favor. Even so, I remind her the doctors expect to take tests after the second treatment to see if the chemo is working, and to take only one treatment aborts the process. She agrees to a second one. I'm relieved, but, again, I'm uneasy as to whether I've done the right thing by her.

On August 6, Barbara's right eye suddenly turns bright red from a ruptured vessel. It scares me until I hear that it's common in people on blood thinners. She takes steroids to counter the brain swelling. The pills puff her cheeks, leave a metallic taste in her mouth, and make her feel shaky at times. Then our radiologist puts her on a pattern of decreasing dosages of both the blood thinners and steroids, hoping to get her off them over the next couple of weeks. Barbara says that it can't come too soon.

She is beginning to sense the inevitability of life ending sooner than she'd like. For years she has been enjoying our good life and wanting to see all our grandchildren grow up. She now weaves back and forth between acceptance and anger about her dying. On occasion, when she's alone, we overhear her let loose with profanities she had learned from her junior high students who lived on the hard streets of Oakland. Her upset saddens us, but we sense it does her good to express it. All the while, she shows uncommon grace to us, the doctors, and everyone who crosses the difficult path she has to walk.

I feel at times as though I am sleepwalking. She's tired and dying, and I'm afraid I won't be worthy of her needs and her love. Looking back, I know these days would have been tougher on both of us had we not taken care of the survival basics I discussed early in part one. For example, our health insurance is adequate, and, though not wealthy, we are not unduly distracted by financial concerns. I also realize, had I not over several decades been observing what dying involves and working on this book, our struggles would have been harder still. And without family and friends who love us, it would have been dreadful, especially for Barbara.

Despite what's in our favor, the pain we feel is terrible enough because both of us are losing her life and our good life together. Being told at seventy-seven that you have a few months to live is easier to bear than hearing the same thing at seventeen, thirty-seven, or even fifty-seven. But it's still painful; Barbara does not want to give up her life, and I certainly don't want to give her up. It is increasingly clear, however, that our long life together, so full of *agape* and worthwhile purpose, pleasure, and joy, is coming to an undesired end. It is a warning to me and our children never to take our health and well-being for granted or forget that one day we too are going to die.

We receive some good news late in August: The cancer markers have dropped from twenty-four to eighteen, which means the chemo is working (the hard goal is the three-to-five range). My heart skips a beat. Is this a sign that the hospital doctors were wrong? Or that they painted an overly pessimistic picture to protect us and themselves? By now, we know we are dealing with something deadly, but this report encourages us and I find myself almost giddy over it. And while there is nothing funny about cancer, this kind of good news helps us maintain our sense of humor, mostly and rightly at my expense. Barbara thinks it's funny that I've been telling friends I've discovered we have a vacuum cleaner, and a dishwasher and oven in our kitchen.

Our doctors tell us to keep life as *normal* as possible without letting it be too strenuous for Barbara. On her best days, she's game for most anything. A few nights before her second round of chemo, we take our turn hosting about thirty neighbors for our monthly block party (people bring finger food to share and their own drinks). The next day, we play in our monthly golf scramble with friends. Barbara rides in the cart with me, keeps score for us, and putts most of the nine holes. For us to score our only *birdie*, she drops an eight-foot putt. Our foursome is awful this day, but I am so proud of her. The week is comparatively good, despite the fact it ends with chemo.

Several days after the second treatment, Barbara feels especially weak. I get her to her oncologist and a blood test reveals anemia, common in chemotherapy patients. On September 10, at the John Muir infusion center, she undergoes a two-pint, five-hour blood transfusion to boost her red blood cells. She is spunkier for a few days. We count this as good, though we can't shake the awareness that her day is drawing nearer.

A week later, the anemia is gone and the cancer marker has dropped to nine. This appears to be further good news—the chemo apparently continues to work. Just the day before, however, Barbara had suffered a few scary episodes of what brain doctors call *cognitive dysfunction*. She became disoriented, briefly losing her ability to speak, and couldn't do things she'd done for years, such as send a simple e-mail. We take her to her oncologist, and she notes that her patient is still very weak. When Barbara tells her she isn't going to take a third chemo treatment, the doctor suggests she forget about it for a week or two until she *regains her strength*, and then, if she wants to slip back into the process, she may.

When driving away from the oncologist's office, we stop at the first traffic light. Barbara puts her hand on my arm and tells me quietly, *I am going to stop the chemo, even if I regain my strength*. I don't know what to say, so I don't say anything. I can tell not only that she knows the decision will shorten her days but also that she wants to live whatever time she has left without the toxic chemicals flooding her bloodstream. She then begins talking about engaging a home hospice program, which brings us both to tears. As I drive carefully the now-familiar route through the streets of Walnut Creek to our home, I cry at her courage. She cries at my love and at the compassion everyone has shown her. We both cry over a looming sense of loss.

During September, conditions are going downhill. And while we presumably have been battling the cancer cells, what has taken much of our time and energy are Barbara's irritating skirmishes with anemia, urinary tract infections, sodium and blood thinning imbalances, and a frustrating ricochet between constipation and diarrhea.

Back in July, the first news of Barbara's condition changes the way we live. I have to learn to do things around the condo she can no longer handle. I have to stop doing some things I enjoy but now don't have time for; and that is perfectly okay. As I say in one of my e-mail reports, rather than regretting these changes I realize that none of my ministries over four decades was more sacred or enriching than that of serving her in this most intimate time. I detest, of course, her disease and my inability to make it go away, but I prize the privilege of doing whatever I can for her. No task is too menial or ignoble if it helps lifts her spirits or gives her comfort. And nothing is more precious than having her tell me she loves me and appreciates what I am doing for her.

Late in September we hear the bad news that the cancer is in her liver. Nurse Barbara knows what this means. Even I am aware of how discouraging it is. Our oldest son, Andrew, had flown from Dallas to be with us for a few days. He, Jacqueline, and I accompany Barbara to meet with her oncologist. Barbara tells her she won't be taking any more chemo. The doctor solemnly confirms her right to that choice and then encourages us to contact Hospice of the East Bay, a highly respected local organization. More embraces and tears. On the way home, the four of us drive to nearby Lafayette for dinner at our favorite Mexican restaurant. Barbara enjoys the food but more importantly appears relieved of that *terrible burden* of choice I referred to earlier.

I worked for several years on the book that in part formed the basis for this one. It includes the section on *dying with dignity* you read in part two. Barbara has seen an earlier draft and, a few nights after declaring her decision for hospice, asks me to read that section to her. You will remember such things as accepting the fact that one day you will die, taking care of unfinished business, dying at home surrounded by loved ones who do their best to keep you from pain, and so on. When I finish reading, she takes my hand, looks at me with eyes that tell me she assumes I can and will do something for her, and says: *That is exactly what I want.*

Within a week, early in October, a counselor and nurse from Hospice of the East Bay come to our condominium to explain how the program works. You'll remember from part two that hospice is not in the business of healing or seeking a cure. It aims to help us keep Barbara comfortable so she can experience what is often referred to as a *gentle crossing*.

At the orientation visit, our nurse says she will visit every Monday and encourages us to call either her or the triage nurses at any time. If we need a doctor, hospice will send one. She counsels us on care giving, provides drugs for Barbara if she has nausea or pain, and instructs us in how to administer them, which is a very simple procedure. She tells us they will provide any medicines Barbara needs, and, if she wants them, a wheelchair and a chair for the shower. If the day comes we can't get her to the shower, the nurse urged us to call hospice, who will send trained people to give her sponge baths in bed. She also suggests that we buy baby monitoring speakers to put in different rooms so we can hear Barbara wherever we are in the condominium. They work beautifully. Over the next few weeks, our hospice workers' compassion, sensitivity, and professional competence comfort Barbara and ease our anxiety. Barbara recognizes these gifts and could not be more pleased. The program is a godsend and we are happy to discover that Medicare will cover it fully.

Our sorrow, of course, continues with Barbara's relentless decline. During early October, she gets up and goes to the table at least once a day to eat for a few minutes. Around mid-month, she becomes confined to bed. While she is generally alert, the slightest things can confuse her and nausea and a nagging cough threaten to upset her. Fortunately, we can relieve both of them quickly with medication. Hospice also supplies us with the morphine for her pain, and though we use it only once or twice, we all are glad to know it's there if needed.

Barbara and I talk of the inevitable a bit more intensely than during the previous three months. My heart continues to break over what strikes us as a terrible reality, but she seems at peace with it all. From the start, she has seen the sad irony of having lung cancer (she never smoked or lived with anyone who did, she always ate responsibly, and she had not suffered any shortness of breath or chest pain). But she never whines. Not once does she ask, *Why me?* She understands what all of us who live a long life would do well to under-stand—that is, that what is more appropriately to ask is, *Why not me?*

Toward the middle of October, Barbara's four sisters fly from Chicago, Philadelphia, and Washington to spend a few days with her. They tell stories, reminisce, and shed tears. I can tell it's a poignant yet wonderful time for all five sisters. When the four say their goodbyes with kisses, embraces, and tears, they know it's the last time they will see Barbara. And Barbara knows.

The next morning, when we are alone together, she draws me close and asks, *What would it take for me to die? Would it happen if I just stopped eating and drinking?* I tell her we don't want her to think about that because she is still able to enjoy family and friends and isn't in any pain. She nods agreement and we cry once again, holding each other and not wanting to let go.

Years before, Barbara and I both signed an advance health care directive, which I, again, urge you to do if you haven't already done so. It says that if we suffer a serious injury or illness and have little prospect of recovering, we want to be kept comfortable but don't want to prolong a meaningless existence through desperate, artificial measures, such as hooking us up to tubes or machines. When we tell the hospice social worker about the directive, she warns us that if Barbara undergoes what we deem an emergency, and we call 9-1-1, the paramedics cannot honor our directive. To cover this base, she supplies us with a Physician Orders for Life-Sustaining Treatment (POLST) form. If Barbara marks it appropriately and signs it, were we to suddenly find her without a pulse and not breathing, doctors and paramedics will not have to resuscitate her and put her on tubal feeding. Aware that in such a case resuscitation and artificial nutrition would mean nothing positive to her—with a high risk of serious brain damage and no cure for her fatal disease—Barbara gladly signs it. We post it prominently in the hall outside our bedroom alongside the sheet listing her medications.

In mid-October, Margo, Keld, and Jacqueline prepare and serve a remarkable pasta dinner at our place for the *God Squad*. The next Sunday evening, about a month before Thanksgiving, our California kids put together an early turkey-with-all-the-trimmings dinner for us, something Barbara had done for them many times on that special November holiday. Barbara is alert and enjoys these celebrations as precious gifts.

As the following week goes by, however, she spends more and more time napping. On the morning of Wednesday, October 22, Jacqueline makes poached eggs on toast for her. She sits up and obviously enjoys it before going back to sleep. But the next day, for the first time, she throws up her breakfast and drifts back to sleep, and her breathing becomes labored. I sit on the bed and rub her head and shoulders. I suspect she's unaware of what I'm doing, but after a few minutes she opens her eyes and asks rather matter-of-factly, *How long is this going to take?* I tell her, *I don't think it will be long.* She nods and then asks, *Will I just go to sleep and not wake up?* I say through my tears, *I think so... and I hope so.* She nods again, and I say, *We will be left behind to miss you.* She replies, with obvious empathy, *I know.* Grace upon grace.

On Sunday morning, our hospice nurse tells us Barbara is now more in a coma than asleep and says her vital signs indicate that it won't be long. She leaves to attend to someone else nearby but comes back late that afternoon. She checks Barbara's signs and confirms her earlier conclusion. An hour later, as she is leaving, she tells us to call her if we have any concerns or questions.

Family members spend the evening taking turns lying beside Barbara, kissing her, wiping her brow, and holding her hand. At about quarter to ten, I get into my pajamas, relieve Margo on the bed, and snuggle beside Barbara for the night. She is lying seemingly at peace on her back. I lay my right hand on her chest to feel her slow breathing and light heartbeat. After a few minutes, I notice that her eyes are slightly open and I see in them the reflection of a recessed light on the bedroom ceiling directly over her. Though it is turned as low as it could go on the dimmer switch, I don't want the light to disturb her or be on all night, so I work my way off the bed, walk all the way around it to the switch on the wall, and turn the light completely off. We are in almost total darkness. I feel my way around the bed, and slip into it again, and put my hand back on Barbara's chest. Her breathing and the beating of her heart are gone. They went, as it were, with the turning out of the light a few minutes after ten o'clock on Sunday night, October 26, 2008.

I call out to family members in the living room. We huddle together by the bed for more embraces and tears. I remind them of our prepaid contracts for cremation with the Nautilus Society. They will take care of the business end of things such as picking up, transporting, and cremating Barbara's remains; reporting her death to the county; and ordering the death certificates. I get out our Nautilus folder with the phone number I've printed in large numbers on the cover, but we we are all exhausted and decide to call them and Hospice of East Bay in the morning. After a while, I lie down next to Barbara for the last time and for a few minutes hold her hand until I turn over and fall asleep.

The last month meant much to our family. Our beloved patient made it through the passage virtually pain free, we had our chance to show her we loved her and to say our good-byes, and the experience drew us closer together. Some important things I think I already knew embedded themselves more deeply in my brain through this process: (1) It *takes a village* to sustain care-giving over months—it's too demanding, intense and constant for one

143

person, no matter how strong he or she is; (2) to discern how not to over- or under-medicate your dying loved one is a night-and-day, heavy responsibility for family members; and (3) I say it once again—we will always do well to maintain deeply respectful relationships not only with family but also with friends, who will enrich our lives and who, when it comes our turn to die, will accompany us through *the valley of the shadow of death.*

If you think about it, you can identify things you do and do not want to happen around your own dying. If you come to terms with the fact it is natural to die, if you do what you can to repair any relationships that are fractured, if you regularly take care of important business matters, if you carry adequate medical insurance so you don't unnecessarily burden your family, and if you are able to be cared for and to die without serious or prolonged pain, then no matter your age, you have a chance of dying with a real measure of dignity. You cannot escape your inevitable death, but you can take actions now that may help you be more at peace when the moment arrives and live your best life before it does.

If you are young or middle aged, it's possible that you may die before living a long life. An accident, disease, war, terrorism, or natural or human-caused disaster may cut your life short. Unless you've lived an unspeakably dreadful life, family and friends will be sad about your ill-timed death, and that sadness will be deepened if they believe you died never having lived your best possible life.

If you are in your later years and have lived robustly, mostly free of serious pain and suffering, you can thank yourself, your loved ones, and competent medical people. You also can count yourself fortunate among our species, which has suffered a lot of pain.

Few of us will have much of a choice when it comes to when and how we die. Some of us will no doubt die unexpectedly and quickly doing something we like to do. I suspect we have all known someone who dropped dead on a golf course, on stage, at a party, at the beach on vacation with family, or even while working. We have all said or heard someone else say, *He died doing what he loved to do.* Our grief is modified by such a realization. We've also known someone who died of old age and never got around to living fully, and that knowledge made us sad.

On Friday morning, November 7, 2008, we hold a memorial gathering for Barbara. More than four hundred family and friends pack the Fireside Room in our Rossmoor Gateway complex. We reminisce, shed tears, and honor and celebrate her life with a beautiful slide-show of photos, songs, poetry, and personal words from those whose lives she touched. At the beginning of the sharing time, Margo has her three brothers and all their children stand together at the front and identifies them as Barbara's most precious legacy. Barbara attended many of the memorial services I created, and she trusted us to do what would nourish the people she cared about. We think she would have loved it.

Good food and drink, conversation, and a relaxed viewing of displays of memorabilia representing Barbara's life follow the scripted memorial hour. That evening, family and close friends crowd into our condo for dinner and further reminiscences. Then they all go home.

I am not left totally alone. My granddaughter, Jacqueline, will live with me for nine months while she volunteers and then gains employment at the University of California in San Francisco's brain center. Although she is gone all day most of the time, she has such a great love for her grandmother and me that she is a good companion when she is home. I impose on her an unwritten agreement that she will stay with me until, for any reason, she decides it would be best to move out or until I kick her out. I will always be grateful for her presence during those months following Barbara's death.

I continue to grieve. I began dealing with grief the moment I heard the ominous CT scan report on the swelling in Barbara's brain. I have long defined grief as *the painful adjustments we must make when faced with an unhappy reality we can't control.* The reality may be small, everyday happenstances such as not being able to find your keys, or it could be more life-altering matters, such as a divorce, the loss of a job, or the death of a person close to you.

Grieving may be simple, but it is not necessarily easy, because it involves heartbreak. You may be best able to attend to what is causing your pain by sitting or lying down and and letting your legitimate emotions have their way with you. For many days over many months, alone in my condominium, I take the time—or my pain makes me take the time—to feel my loss and to express my sadness through sobbing.

The main point I want to make here is that time does not *heal all wounds*; expressing your grief does. I stress this in the last chapter of *Too Nice for Your Own Good* after I tell of my mother's sudden death as I am finishing high school. I identify it as *probably the worst day of my life*. So I know how painful grieving can be. I also know it's extremely important for my well-being that I don't fight it or pretend I'm above it. I'm aware that we all grieve in our own way and at our own pace. I also know I can expect to endure common expressions of sadness, emotional lack of control, and depression.

Grieving in public can be especially difficult. Your emotions may take over when you least want them to. On several occasions, when out and about, I find myself on the brink of tears, or actually crying and making others uncomfortable, which I don't like to do. They want to protect me from my grief; and, ironically, I want to protect them from it. And each time I'm tempted to do this, I remember another important point I discuss in *Too Nice for Your Own Good:* Our task is not to *protect* people from their grief but to *support* them through it.

Grieving may also be hard because it often involves anger. Even when we're aware of our anger and know its causes, we're not sure how to process it helpfully. We know it's unhealthy to repress it forever, to dump it on those who don't deserve it, or to rage against those who do, but because we don't know how to express it constructively, anger scares most of us. In Chapter 3 of *Too Nice for Your Own Good*, I describe how you can release your anger in ways that are honest but that won't hurt your important relationships at work or at home.

You will find it especially difficult to grieve if you have tried to establish a reputation for being tough. *Macho* men often have trouble letting their painful emotions out even in private; they tend to interpret being emotional as a weakness, indicating they are not the strong persons they pretend to be. I feel fortunate that I don't need to maintain a macho image and can grieve freely.

Of all the negative, painful aspects of my loss, the two that broadside me are (1) a most profound sense of solitude, even when with others, and (2) the finality of it all—the terrible fact that Barbara, whom I loved and whose presence made me feel complete, is no longer with me. When leading memorial services, I always name the person who died and say that she or he is gone, that he or she still will be with us in influence and in memory but will not be present as in the past. In my head, I know this is true and important for us all to recognize. In dying, we go away and do not come back. I have felt this truth with some pain when good friends have died. But when Barbara dies, as when my mother died, I experienced it as emotionally devastating. In the first few months, the fact that Barbara is permanently gone lay heavy on my heart. Sobbing gave me a sense of release. It also left me feeling weak and exhausted at times.

In the first months after Barbara's death, I unconsciously and typically try to ease my grief, if not run away from it, by keeping busy. After the death of a spouse, the one left behind must deal with a lot of financial, insurance, tax, and other time consuming business matters. I tackle such things conscientiously. But just when I think the busywork will help me not to think about my loss, the very matter I am working on reminds me of it.

In early December, I begin writing my memoir. It is another unconscious attempt, I suppose, to occupy my mind and get me through my grief with less pain. By April 2009, I have ground out two hundred pages, including photos. I am writing so that my children, grandchildren, and closest friends will remember me a bit better after I'm gone. I still work on it from time to time.

As if that's not enough, in April, with the hardest months of my grieving behind me, I throw myself into founding the Drama Association of Rossmoor. I love theater and it has bothered me for years that in our retirement community, with over two hundred organizations, not one of them promotes live theater or offers guided play-writing, acting, or stage craft lessons. I corral a couple of friends and they collect a few of theirs who love the theater, and we form a steering committee. By our third meeting, we have clarified what we think a drama organization might do and begun to plan a gala kickoff party for Saturday night June 27. At the party, we will explain what we are about, inform everyone about local theater groups (some will be there to entertain us), offer a few drama programs of our own, and recruit formal members. As the chair, I take the responsibility to plan the big party and *work my tail off*, so to speak.

This leads me to the second postscript.

The Royal Oak of High Eagle Ridge

Anointed overseer and caregiver
Of your devoted parishioners
We met under your tortured boughs years ago.
And promised to be friends and neighbors forever.

First, whimsical Paul, who
Would break out in song in odd moments,
Now silent.

One by one we are slipping away.
My beloved centered Sylvia, whose ashes
Were strewn at your roots for added sustenance.

Then saintly Barbara, whose gentle crossing,
Surrounded by love, was preordained,
Leaving an unfillable void.

Paula, knowledgeable about all living creatures,
Large and small, who inhabit the earth,
Fought bravely for survival to the bitter end.

And Ro, wheelchair bound,
Never relinquished her zeal for life,
Lived it to the end.

Russell, hermit-like and fragile,
Living and passing, then gone,
Had a mind filled with professional insight.

Fun-loving Bill, with sharp barbs,
Knew everyone's vulnerability and exploited it.
Keen of wit, and lover of malt nectar, gone.

Several more seem to evaporate
Before I ever got to know them.
Their shadows remain, but they are no longer with us.

You stand on your throne-like elevation,
Immutable, silently observing,
Unable to stop mere mortals from one by one slipping away.

The forms and shapes and manners of all
Are becoming fleeting memories,
Slowly fading, drifting, drifting.

I often wonder what brought me here
To these glorious hills where eagles soar
And the ever-brilliant sun lightens the twilight of my years.

Why has time, once plentiful and joyous,
Become an inexorable enemy?
Life has become an exquisite lottery,
Winners and losers to the inevitable end.

How painful to observe this human erosion.
And you Royal Oak, standing aloof
Must be the keeper of their souls,
A blending of nature and humanity.

Shall I rage or revolt, or accept the inevitable
And yield to the master timekeeper —
Not yet. I think I'll have another cup of coffee.

Ben Slomoff   January 22, 2011

Because of its tremendous solemnity death is the light in which great passions, both good and bad, become transparent, no longer limited by outward appearances.

Soren Kierkegaard

Death is a very dreary affair, and my advice is to have nothing whatsoever to do with it.

Somerset Maugham

The dark background which death supplies brings out the tender colors of life in all their purity.

George Santayana

Remembering that I'll be dead soon is the most important tool I've ever encountered to help me make the big choices in life.

Steve Jobs

PERSONAL POSTSCRIPT TWO

I write here about my serious brush with death in the summer of 2009.

Without Barbara, I settle into my new life at Rossmoor. Moving away never enters my mind. I count the place home and am happy and grateful to be here. In the first couple of months, I think little of any future companion; I'm too busy grieving and actually can't imagine anyone replacing Barbara. I've been warned about the *casserole brigade*. Male friends tell me there are four single women to every single man in Rossmoor. There is an in-house assumption that single women flock after new widowers. The *brigade* is a myth. Were it real, I think I should interpret the fact that I never experienced it, as rejection.

In late January, at a dinner meeting, I am introduced by a mutual friend to a woman whose first husband, a Presbyterian minister, took her twenty-five years ago to a Sunday celebration at the Montclair Church where I was pastor. He died several years ago; she had remarried and her second husband has died in the past month. We share the pain and loneliness of losing a love and decide it would be nice to have dinner together sometime. I call her a week or two later and we have a good time. We do it again and both of us, I think, have another pleasant evening, but we are still too new at grieving and are not interested in starting a serious relationship.

In April each year, our tennis club throws a festive dinner party called the Spring Fling. Barbara and I went every year. This year my daughter, Margo, is my *date* and we sit with friends right in front of the stage, the perfect place for me to take lots of photos of the various colorful song-and-dance routines based on Beatles music. It is a visual hoot. My photos turn out well, so I e-mail various shots to friends whose antics on stage I had captured. I then put the album online so that other tennis club members can see them and buy any copies they'd like. I buy a lot of them.

For several years, Claire Blue has created the entertainment routines we enjoy at the Spring Fling, always carefully organizing them and creatively involving as many tennis club people as practicable. I've known Claire for eight years and, for five years prior to Barbara's illness, the two of them played tennis together on Thursday mornings. In 2005, Barbara and I went a few times to see Jinna Davis, a tennis club member who was housebound and dying of breast cancer. It impressed us each time we visited, that Claire either was making Jinna's lunch, playing dominoes with her or giving her a back rub. I remember our coming home, shaking our heads, and reflecting, *Isn't it wonderful that Claire is such a great friend to Jinna?*

For a month or two, a couple of good mutual tennis club friends are independently and separately speaking to her and to me about our getting together, or *dating*. I have always thought of Claire as attractive, bright, lots of fun, and a very good person, but I am not in a rush to be involved with anyone.

A couple of Claire's friends who bought my photos online show them to her (she doesn't have or want a computer). They make a point of telling me she really likes the pictures and urge me to get together with her to show her the whole album. I am swamped with the Drama Association but decide that when I can get a break, I will give Claire a call. Like any photographer, I feel good when people make a fuss over my pictures.

The second week in May, I call Claire and ask if she'd like to go to dinner, with the idea that I'd bring the photos with me. She says yes. We have a good time, and I give her the prints. I also toss out the idea that maybe we could do the dinner thing again. Some days later, I remember hearing her say she loves the violin and notice that the critically claimed movie *The Violinist* is playing nearby. She seems pleased with the idea of dinner and seeing that movie, and we both enjoy another good evening.

The next Saturday morning, I take the nearly two-hour drive to Roseville to see two of my grandsons play baseball. I stay over night and leave early on Sunday to get back to the Rossmoor tennis courts for an eleven o'clock memorial gathering for one of our tennis players who, after suffering depression for years, finally succeeded in taking her own life. I want to attend the memorial. On the drive home, however, I am surprised to realize I also am very much looking forward to seeing Claire, whom I assume will be there. We end up connecting after the memorial and walking down the path from the courts to the parking lot together. She seems as comfortable with me as I am with her.

After my having been the *official unofficial photographer* for the Spring Fling, Claire sends me an invitation to a cast party on May 27. She is in charge of it and, again, I am pleased to see her. After another dinner out, I tell her I like being with her and that I sensed she is pleased to see me, but I want her to know I am not in a hurry to be serious with anyone and want to take things very slowly. She understands, and says she feels the same way.

Then one afternoon in early June, while emptying the dishwasher, I feel what I take to be a muscle spasm in my lower back (I've had many back spasms over the years). Two weeks later, I am on drugstore painkillers and stressed out, feverishly planning that big June 27 gala kickoff party for the Drama Association. Then, three nights in a row, on June 18, 19, and 20, I attend Rossmoor dinner parties—one with Margo, and two with Claire—and I medicate myself each night with bourbon for pain. I count this an emergency remedy and tell myself I will see my primary care physician as soon as I am through the Drama Association's big shindig the next weekend.

All this leads to Sunday morning, June 21—Father's Day. I get out of bed and lie on the floor with several pillows to support my back, hoping to ease the now-excruciating pain. My granddaughter, Jacqueline, still lives with me but has flown to Philadelphia for the weekend, and Margo is in Roseville. With the pain getting worse, I call Claire from the floor with a mobile phone. Even with her help I can't stand up, so she calls Margo. With no Sunday morning traffic, Margo makes the nearly two-hour drive in record time. When she can't get me up, she calls 9-1-1.

Paramedics haul me in an ambulance to the E.R. at John Muir Hospital, where Barbara was treated a year earlier. After hearing my history of muscle spasms and doing some tests, they send me home with painkillers and muscle relaxants. The next night, someone calls from John Muir to tell me I need to be admitted to the hospital the next morning because my problem is not a muscle spasm but a methicillin-resistant staphylococcus aureus (MRSA, pronounced *mersa*), a deadly bacterial staph infection that resists antibiotics. I have never heard of such a thing.

I go back to John Muir the next morning, impressed with the fact I have contracted something serious but not knowing what to expect. An MRI reveals that a relatively small but ugly abscess has formed on the base of my spine. My doctors, including an orthopedic surgeon, decide not to operate but to put me on infusions of a strong antibiotic. They do this despite the aggressive nature and power of this infection because of the small size of the abscess and the always risky procedures of spinal surgery. Their decision pleases me.

My infectious disease doctors immediately put me on the strong painkiller, Diladid, and on vancomycin, the gold standard antibiotic for MRSAs. When I ask how long my hospital stay will be, they tell me three or four days and I think to myself, *I can handle that*. But the nasty infection proves stubborn. I'm there ten days. Nothing about this pleases me. It means that on June 27, the night of the Drama Association huge kickoff party, for which I'd *worked my tail off*, I'm flat on my abscessed *tail* in the hospital. I also learn during my stay that people die from MRSAs, even when treated properly. I decide not to worry about missing the party.

How did I get the infection? My nurse tells me people usually pick them up in hospitals, but I tell her I haven't been near one for a year. She then says they are becoming epidemic outside of hospitals. I suspect a lingering, irritated spider bite near my right knee. My doctors say they can't be sure how it entered my system. It doesn't matter; so far it hasn't killed me. I feel fortunate.

My Northern California kids and friends, including Claire, visit me. When she goes away for four days on a long-planned trip with girlfriends to Cambria, four hours down the California coast, she borrows a cell phone and calls me. Despite difficulty with the phone cutting in and out, her persistence in getting through and the concern in her voice further endear her to me. When she returns, she comes to see me immediately.

I lose eleven pounds in the ten days I spend in John Muir, which when released I try to gain back by eating ice cream, fettuccine Alfredo, ice cream, avocado, ice cream, cinnamon buns, yogurt to replenish the good bacteria killed by the antibiotic, and more ice cream. I gain that weight back in a couple of weeks, all the while bravely suffering the intake.

Before I leave the hospital, my doctors insert a PICC line—a *port*, into my left underarm. It runs through an artery up over my left shoulder and down to just above my heart. Moving the infused antibiotic close to my heart disburses the medication throughout my system faster than an injection in my wrist. And having the port means I don't have to be stuck with a needle twice a day for the next six weeks. I take it as a good thing.

Also, while I am still in the hospital, the infectious disease team tests various antibiotics with my MRSA. Daptomycin has a good immediate showing, so it is the drug of choice. At home, I quickly grow accustomed to infusing myself twice a day through the port, but it is not all fun—there is constipation, an upset stomach from pills, and a killer bladder infection. I also am foggier than usual from the drugs. These things will pass, and I assume they are worth it to kill the infection.

Each week, when I pick up a new antibiotic supply, the doctors check the line to see that it's sterilized and working properly. But as weeks pass, the ongoing pain is not decreasing. The line is working, but I'm not sure the Daptomycin is. I don't want to be a crybaby, but as we face the fifth week of infusions I mention the pain to my doctors and they order an MRI. The scan shows that the abscess has not abated but has enlarged and gotten worse.

The next week, now almost two months after first entering John Muir, I return for a major back operation. It's August 13, and I'm hoping the date will prove lucky. Before the surgery, I am fitted for a turtle-shell type back brace that they tell me I'll wear at least for the next four months. Once on the table and sedated, and my surgeon has gotten to the base of my spine, he cuts out the worst of the abscessed bone, puts two screws into each of my fourth and fifth lumbar, and anchors them to a metal bar. He then mixes a protein epoxy with a powder made from grinding a piece of my pelvic bone he cut out and, in some way, uses it to glue the lumbar together (at least this is what my medically untrained mind remembers of his explanation afterward). Once back in my room, the nurses keep me comfortable for seven days of recovery. Toward the end of that week, I am feeling pretty good. I also am sick of being bedridden and am really looking forward to leaving John Muir.

The day before I am to go home, however, my surgeon finds pockets of pus under the six-inch incision that now runs the length of my lower spine. He tells me I will have another MRI that night, and adds that regardless of the results I must undergo a second operation the next evening. The procedure will not be as invasive as the first, he assures me, while acknowledging it still is delicate spine surgery. I have been super ready to go home and don't like the idea that the first operation didn't work. A loss of hope for defeating the infection is beginning to eke its way into the back of my mind.

I am increasingly both impressed and depressed by the power of the MRSA. During my first hospitalization in June, it took three times longer than they expected for the vancomycin to get it under control. When I went home and administered twice-daily doses of the promising Daptomycin for five weeks, the infection dominated it, rendering it impotent. Back in the hospital, an operation designed not only to help repair and strengthen my back but also to kill the infection at its root, plus an intense week of post-surgery antibiotic infusions geared to finish it off, failed.

When my surgeon explains the second operation to *wash out* the infection, he tells me that if it doesn't do the trick, he can operate a third time, going in through the front. I don't like the thought of a third operation, let alone the part about going in *through the front*. I have heard enough about him to be impressed with him, his reputation, and his commitment to solve my medical problem. And I know he wants to encourage me with this news. But I also am reminded, as I mentioned earlier, that medicine is not an exact science, and that doctors are not gods. He, in company with my infectious disease team are portraying their work here as a very difficult battle, without giving me the confidence they can win it.

I accept the idea of the second, less extensive operation to *wash out* the deadly bacteria—I am right there in the hospital and, actually, they give me the impression I don't have a choice. So I submit without a fight. After they strap me in a gurney, Margo and her girls, Jacqueline and Christina, sit with me through the prep time and accompany me to the operating room door, at which time I notice tears glistening in their eyes. It is a sweet and sincere gesture that I cherish, but it does make me wonder if they know something I don't. I flash on my pastoral practice when routinely calling on church members in the hospital–I'd immediately say something that would assure them I wasn't there because their doctors told me they weren't going to make it.

For the first few days and nights after the second surgery, when we still are not sure it will work, I find myself lying awake pondering my options if it doesn't. I see them as two: One, submit to a third, more invasive, scarey sounding spinal surgery, even as my confidence in anyone's ability to conquer this nasty infection is fading.

Two, refuse the frontal operation and for the rest of my life take antibiotics of my doctors' choice. I realize this option also holds no real promise of victory over the MRSA, but nothing they have tried so far has done that, and it will save me going through more spinal surgeries and prolonged recoveries in the hospital. I learned early on that MRSAs readily kill people. It now dawns on me that I may be determining how and approximately when I will die. It also strikes me that I never before have come this close to deciding on such life-and-death realities having to do with me.

At some point, while going back and forth between these options, I settle on turning down the third operation *through the front*. And I find myself relieved. I am so impressed by what Hospice of the East Bay did for Barbara and what it meant to me and my family, that I am at peace with the prospect of turning myself over to them no matter how soon the time might come. I decide that if follow-up tests show that the second operation hasn't been successful, I will talk with my doctors and explain my decision. I suspect they will feel it's too soon for such a choice and will try to talk me out of it. But I'm not afraid to face them. I feel as Barbara had felt–I have had a long, interesting and satisfying life; and I have no need to extend it with debilitating measures that promise neither freedom from unnecessary or uncontrollable suffering nor healthy opportunities to enjoy family and friends.

I don't believe I could or should have made this choice at thirty-six or fifty-six. At seventy-six, I'm a bit surprised at how easily it comes to me. I also can't imagine making such a decision at seventy-six before that savage back pain hit me just a couple of months before. Now, with the several failed efforts to kill the infection, I have come to accept the fact I may die fairly soon. I have long ago killed the grim reaper for me, by dismissing him as a negative myth, by seeing my dying as the last natural act of my living, by putting off any fear of a dreadful afterlife, and by trusting in perfect love. While not afraid of my doctors, I realize I don't want to let Claire know what I have decided. She later tells me I hinted at it, and we both got tears in our eyes. And I certainly don't want to tell my kids (my son, Steve, whose mother's dying not ten months earlier remains painfully embedded in his consciousness, told Claire, *If my father dies, I'll kill him*.) So I don't say a word. I figure time will tell.

Claire's affection during my first hospital stay dramatically sped up the deepening of our relationship, the one we intended to take so *very* slowly. I now am aware that I'm in love with her (remember that section on falling in love in part one?) and that being with her profoundly enriches my life. I also am feeling sorry for her in that I was the one who made the overtures for us to see each other, and five minutes after we both realize something could develop between us, I land in the hospital with a life-threatening illness. There's no doubt it's our love and the prospect of being together that has gotten me through medicine's inability to assure me we can defeat the MRSA. I have made a choice. I am not convinced I will get well, but I very much want to. I look forward to recovering and, if that doesn't happen, to spending whatever time I have left close to her.

As you have deduced, the second operation to *wash out* the infection works. I am released from John Muir, September 1, 2009, and spend fifteen days in Manor Care just outside Rossmoor for rehabilitation and more antibiotic infusions (that makes it seven weeks in medical facilities). I'm tired of being institutionalized, but as I walk the halls to strengthen my leg and back muscles, I am struck by how fortunate I am compared to most others who must remain there. I can't help but recall Denis Waitley's words: *I had the blues because I had no shoes, until upon the street I meet a man who had no feet.*

I go home to infuse myself with vancomycin twice a day for a month before switching to sulfa tablets, which I am to take orally morning and night for six more months. My doctors tell me the antibiotics have a hard time defeating bacteria that cling to metal, such as the screws and bars holding my lumbar together, and the MRSA could flare up again if the sulfa doesn't reach them all. I realize I am not out of the woods, and it may be a rather long haul because the risk of the infection reigniting is serious. But I am happy to be home, healing and looking forward to a possible full recovery.

Over the next few months, the infusions diminish the infection, the bones in my back are able to start healing and I am regaining my strength. I will wear the turtle-shell body brace well into 2010, I am told. The surgical scar is tender and I am not to lift more than five pounds. I cannot do my wash, go shopping, prepare my meals, put my socks on or tie my shoelaces (the brace won't let me bend). My two local children, Margo and Steve, have their own work and families to take care of, so while they are helpful when they can be, they can't be on the scene hour-by-hour, day in and day out. Claire takes care of these things for me. She lovingly drives me to doctors and labs, to the bank, to the store, and to wherever I need or want to go. In so many ways, she makes life so much more than bearable.

My infectious disease doctors inform me that when I have finished the six months of sulfa, I'll have two options: (1) Keep on taking it for the rest of my life, or (2) stop taking it and see what happens (which they recommend). This second option has two advantages: I wouldn't be overloading my body with a drug that could have long-term, negative side effects, and I wouldn't have to worry about remembering to take that damned pill twice a day.

When I will stop the sulfa in March 2010, the odds stand at fifty–fifty that any bacteria still attached to the metal could reignite the infection, probably within two to four weeks. If this doesn't happen, the fight is over, which is the wonderful outcome we want. If it does (I'll know it by pain and fever), my surgeon will go in, remove the screws and put me back on antibiotic infusions for a month, hoping, once again, that they will finish off the infection. This is not as major a procedure as when he put them in, and he won't go in *through the front*, but it will be another operation on my spine, nonetheless. And once again, I'm given the impression I don't have a say in the matter.

In January 2010, the sulfa is controlling and perhaps eradicating the infection and I'm told I only need to take it for a few more months (hooray!). X-rays show that my back is stable and the bones are healing, which means I can stop wearing the back brace (hooray!). I need physical therapy but should soon be able to get back to a normal life, including, by March, even tennis and golf (hooray!). So, aside from the shadow of the possible return of the infection in the fall, I feel very good and very fortunate. Physically, I feel just about the way I did before those nasty bacteria abscessed on my spine the previous May.

In February, however, I experience a sudden outbreak of ugly red blotches all over my torso. A biopsy shows it's the sulfa, so my doctors shift me to doxycycline, an antibiotic related to the popular tetracycline. They also decide I should stay on it for another six months into September 2010, a full year from the spinal operations, which means a probable delay of any surgery until the fall. I see this as a glitch—perhaps a pain in the... *spine,* but not a major setback.

Over the summer, thinking of a possible operation doesn't thrill me, but I am living with a new love in my life. Then, September arrives, and I stop taking the doxycycline. Nothing happens. Nothing happens in October. Nothing happens in November. It was a hard eighteen months, but we stopped the infection and now, a year later, I apparently have recovered fully. For that, I credit my dilligent, skilled and careful physicians, who didn't give up on me. Also, for restoring my spirit, I thank my children; my grandchildren and my dear friends, whose love I was aware of through it all. And I am, of course, deeply grateful to Claire—I don't think I would have made it without her.

Skip forward to November 2011, when this book goes to the printer. Claire and I continue to live together. She has back problems of her own. She had unsuccessful surgery forty years ago, was on disability for nine years, and still has to visit her chiropractor twice a week to get through her days. For a year now, she's been unable to play tennis or golf. At seventy-two, staying well enough to be physically active is not easy, but, with the help of a retired, orthopedic surgeon friend, she's working to strengthen her *core*. *She's* also gone through a decompression and laser treatment program. And she has me.

I've turned seventy-eight and I feel it, but there still are no signs of the MRSA. In October 2010, playing tennis a bit recklessly, I took a nasty spill and broke my clavicle. I have gotten back into that game and golf, playing them as well and as poorly as I ever have, though at a bit slower pace...and more carefully. I'm trying to be smarter. And I have Claire to help me.

I have an unwritten agreement with her that she will not die before me—I prefer not to go through the kind of awful loss and grief I suffered in 2008–09. Of course, as I point out in part two, we don't have complete control over when, how, or where we will die. Right now, both of us feel fortunate to have love in the twilight of our years and look forward to whatever future we may enjoy together. Having come to better terms with dying, despite physical ailments we are committed to living our best possible life.

Claire joins me in wishing you the same good prospect.

ACKNOWLEDGEMENTS

The perspectives in this book emerged in my mind over the past half-century. Specific sources are hard to identify due to the passing of time, the broad spectrum of my reading, and the fact I see myself mainly as a translator and applier of insights from others. I can tell you that the ancient Hebrew prophets, Socrates and other Greek philosophers, and, obviously, Jesus and the Gospel writers profoundly shaped my worldview.

I owe a debt of gratitude to the late Fuller seminary professor Edward John Carnell, who a long time ago taught me to think and steered me into critical areas of self-reflection I otherwise would have avoided. He also introduced me to the eighteenth-century Danish Christian existentialist Soren Kierkegaard, who also made an impact on my worldview.

My agent on my first book, Laurie Harper, who now bills herself as an authors' consultant on the business aspects of publishing, was there for me when I needed information and support. Closer to home, my longtime friend, colleague, and patient editor, John Hadsell, helped immeasurably with his questions and wise observations.

For support through the early development of this book, I note the affirmation of my wife, Barbara. For encouraging me to finish it and get it published in 2011, I am indebted to Claire Blue. (You read about these wonderful women in the postscripts.)

My gratitude also goes to the *God Squad* : Vernon and Gloria Alexander, Dale and Elsie Cooper, Paul and Eleanor Gertmenian, John and Virginia Hadsell, Norm and Enid Pott, and Dean and Dorothy Skanderup, all of whom saw early, partial, if not full drafts of the book and whose longtime friendship, support, and encouragement I cherish.

I thank Rossmoor friends Eric Anschutz, Bobbie Frankel and Richard Golden, whom I quote, and Jane Walters, all of whom read drafts of material and whose input improved the book. My gratitude also goes to the medical and academic professionals, whose names appear on the back cover, for having read the manuscript and commended it so highly.

I also gratefully acknowledge the four poems by neighbor and friend Ben Slomoff that grace the pages between major sections of the book. *When Life Ends*, which sits before the first personal postscript, was written the day after Barbara died and was read at her memorial gathering. *The Royal Oak of High Eagle Ridge,* which appears in front of the second postscript, pays tribute to the majestic 350 year old tree that stands on a knoll just above our condominium. Ben recounts the number of neighbors he has known on High Eagle Court who have died over the past few years, including his wife, Sylvia, and Barbara, and pays tribute to this stately oak that stands as an observer of our comings and goings. We look forward to the prospect of celebrating Ben's one hundredth birthday on November 16, 2013.

THE AUTHOR

Duke Robinson identifies himself as a writer. Time Warner published the paperback version of his award-winning book in November 2000, under the title *Too Nice for Your Own Good: How to Stop Making 9 Self-Sabotaging Mistakes*. It appeared in eleven languages and, in English, as an e-book and an audiotape and remains available through Amazon.com and bookstores everywhere. A third book, entitled, *SAVIOR: An Old Notion in a New Novel of Unthinkable Absurdity*, is scheduled for publication in 2012.

Robinson was born and reared in the Philadelphia area, where many of his relatives still abide. He has lived the last half-century in the East Bay of Northern California. For twenty-eight years, he served as pastor of the progressive Montclair Presbyterian Church in Oakland. For several years during that ministry, he served as an adjunct professor at San Francisco Theological Seminary, from which he holds an earned doctorate. Prior to retiring he was known widely as a speaker and appeared frequently on television in Northern California.

Since 2000, the author has lived in Rossmoor, an active adult community in Walnut Creek, California. Barbara, his wife of fifty-four years died in 2008. He tells the story of her suddenly discovered illness and her dying in the first personal postscript of this book. He has four children and nine grandchildren.

Made in the USA
Charleston, SC
23 February 2012